PARALLEL UNIVERSES:
THE STORY OF REBIRTH

DEAR KAREN,

I'm DELIGHTED THAT OUR UNIVERSES CONVERGED!

PARALLEL UNIVERSES:
THE STORY OF REBIRTH

IN GRATITUDE

David B. Bohl

David B. Bohl

MANY SORSE
04-23-18

Henschel
HAUS
publishing, inc.
Milwaukee, Wisconsin

Published by
HenschelHAUS Publishing, Inc.
www.HenschelHAUSbooks.com

HenschelHAUS titles may be purchased in bulk for educational,
business, fundraising, or promotional use. For information, please
email info@henschelhausbooks.com

PB ISBN: 978159598-578-1
E-book ISBN: 978159598-579-8
Publisher's Cataloging-In-Publication Data
(Prepared by The Donohue Group, Inc.)

Names: Bohl, David B.
Title: Parallel universes : the story of rebirth / David B. Bohl.
Description: Milwaukee, Wisconsin : HenschelHaus Publishing,
Inc., [2018]
Identifiers: ISBN 9781595985781 | ISBN 9781595985798 (ebook)
Subjects: LCSH: Bohl, David B. | Adoptees--Biography.
Adoptees--Mental health. | Alcoholics--Biography.
Alcoholics--Rehabilitation. | LCGFT: Autobiographies.
Classification: LCC HV874.82.B64 A3 2018 | DDC 362.734092--dc23

Cover design by Melissa Lee Johnson, Express Creative
Author photo: Jessica Kaminski, The Refinery Photo Studio

Dedication

*To all who yearn for real connection,
especially those seekers who have had
their quests interrupted by unexpected
and debilitating phenomena.*

"Real isn't how you are made," said the Skin Horse. "It's a thing that happens to you. When a child loves you for a long, long time, not just to play with, but REALLY loves you, then you become Real."

"Does it hurt?" asked the Rabbit.

"Sometimes," said the Skin Horse, for he was always truthful. "When you are Real you don't mind being hurt."

"Does it happen all at once, like being wound up," he asked, "or bit by bit?"

"It doesn't happen all at once," said the Skin Horse. "You become. It takes a long time. That's why it doesn't happen often to people who break easily, or have sharp edges, or who have to be carefully kept. Generally, by the time you are Real, most of your hair has been loved off, and your eyes drop out and you get loose in the joints and very shabby. But these things don't matter at all, because once you are Real you can't be ugly, except to people who don't understand."

–from *The Velveteen Rabbit* by Margery Williams Bianco

Table of Contents

Foreword i

Prologue xxi

The Box 1

Freedom 5

The Lake 8

Parallel Universes 12

A New Life 25

I'm Not Like Them 29

Shy 39

I Hope Someone Out There Will Find Me 47

Pressure 51

Fun 56

Disappointing 63

Evidence 68

Still Not Here 79

The Wolf of the Chicago Board Options Exchange ... 91

Love 94

Life and Death 103

What Is Real? 109

Selling My Soul 112

A Driving Problem 117

The Rest of My Life 119

Golden Ticket 125

Ease and Comfort 130
Criterion Number 5 137
Sailing 144
More Fun 159
The Box Reopened... 165
Broken Hearts 172
My Name is David 181
Sober Now 186
Immersing... 188
Perception 194
Changes 198
Regrets 200
Luck and Strength 205
Lost and Found 209
Moving On 212
My Reality 215
God 219
False Consensus Effect 223
The New World 227
Getting It 233
Pain 235
There's Nothing Wrong With You 245
Safety 251
A Bridge 254
Phenomenal 258
Club Limbic 260
Not a TV Show 264
Freedom 269
Acknowledgments... 271
About the Author... 272

Foreword

What was David's shame? Essentially, it was his sense of not belonging. He was adopted at the age of seven days by loving and caring parents. From the quiet tragedy of his young mother, not yet 21 when she delivered him and gave him up, the salvation was immediate when he became a part of a family that was able to provide for him and give him life that was full of love and attention. It was a "salvation," quite literally, as David was a child of an unwed couple in a time and place where he would be considered a "bastard," a result of "sin." But even though he got saved and was taken into a family that saw him as its own, he still grew up feeling different.

His life wasn't bad at all. There were no major disturbances; he wanted for nothing. Yet, he's always felt that there was something wrong with him. The shame followed him wherever he went. How long has it been with him? The first time when, at the age of six, he told his friends he was adopted and how badly they reacted? Or even earlier than that, before he could even name what it was?

Gabor Maté, a prominent Canadian physician with a special interest in child development, trauma, and the treatment of addiction, says, "Shame is a sense of unworthiness. What [does] the infant think or feel implicitly when a mother leaves him? Infants are narcissists; they think the world is about them—and when they're being abandoned, they feel unworthy. It's not a thought. It's a deep sense of not mattering. Here's the thing that has nothing to do with what [David] told his friends—it's only that the way his friends reacted reinforced the shame inside him. So the shame is already in. You can shame a nine-month-old baby."

David acknowledges that the maladaptive schemas (patterns of thought or behavior that organize categories of information and the relationships among them) he has developed since childhood have kept him in secrecy and discontentment. The fact that he has lived with such burdens since infancy means these patterns haven't been easy to eliminate because they are…inherent. David says, "That's why adoptees and persons with trauma cannot just *think* their way out of the discomfort." Furthermore, David recalls, "I was always feeling less-than, and always entering life situations by adapting to them so as not to be found out and rejected."

* * * * *

Shame affects all areas of self. It can shape our thinking, how we react to the world. It's an emotion that has an external presentation—it is almost impossible to hide it when we feel shame. Picture a scolded child or an adult confronted about a lie. They don't look you in the eye; they are looking away or looking down. There's a reason we manifest shame in that way, why we look away.

Maté says, "It's an over-activation of a certain part of a nervous system. It's a submission. The nervous system has three parts. There's the voluntary nervous system, which is volitional: *I can pick up a thing I want to pick up, I can put it down.* There's another part called "autonomic"—it's not volitional: we don't control our breathing, our heart rate, contortion of our intestines and so on. There are two parts to it: sympathetic (tension, movement) and parasympathetic (relaxation). The two have to be in balance. Shame is an over-activation of the parasympathetic nervous system and it's a response to separation. So if a mother and an infant look into each other's eyes at nine months of age, and the mother looks away, the infant eventually goes into a shame state: *I give up.* The nine-month-old baby has no concept of having done anything wrong; fundamentally, shame is a response to separation."

Maté says, "[David] has felt shame since birth—it kept growing and growing and every time he did something wrong, it added to his sense of shame but the shame was *always* in him. Even with his life's achievements, he was trying to make himself worthy, valuable, because he didn't value himself. "

When at the age of six David revealed his past—that he was adopted—to some friends, he was first confronted with the *inherent* trauma that ailed his psyche. The friends reacted in disbelief; they looked at him as if he was a pariah. Little David tried desperately to convince them that he was "normal," just like them and that being adopted was no big deal. He brought them to his house to get his mother to verify who he was, to explain that there was nothing wrong with him. But the friends disregarded the explanation, the attempt of his mother to smooth things over. They left his house and left him behind. And because of these reactions, it became clear to David that being adopted *was* a big deal. It was a disturbing finding, but he could finally put that inherent state of shame—that most likely originated from being given up for adoption— into words and understanding. Here was the evidence: there really was something wrong with him; he was indeed different than everyone else.

Was there relief in having his difference acknowledged and pointed out by the world? We do sometimes feel relief when we can finally name that which lives unnamed in us. For little David, that confirmation and discovery of shame was devastating. At the same time, as one motivational quote has it: "The pain you feel today is the strength you feel tomorrow. For every challenge encountered is the opportunity for growth." Today, David says that once he was able to identify his pain, eventually—much later in life—he was able to do something about it. He had developed an identity that he could live with in the real world.

* * * * *

Before David started to confront and address his fears, he discovered he could numb his pain and uncertainty by drinking and getting drunk. This—albeit temporarily— brought him some respite; it helped him to cope with his feelings, or at least ignore them. Over time, his drinking escalated, became a necessity. Later in life, David identified as an alcoholic. Easier to diagnose than shame, alcoholism is something that lends itself to more obvious treatment (rehab, 12-step meetings) and David sought treatment. He got sober.

But what about shame? David still felt it. Even in the rooms of Alcoholics Anonymous (AA), even when he was conquering his addiction. He felt isolated in the very environment, AA, that helped him get better. He struggled with the spiritual part of the program; he couldn't find the *power greater than himself* (many sober alcoholics accept *God* as their higher power), which is one of the major tenets of the 12 steps. David continued to feel fragmented, even rejected, by the very program that was saving his life.

* * * * *

A study by Kenneth S. Kendler, *Genetic and Familial Environmental Influences on the Risk for Drug Abuse*, found that "4.5 percent of adopted individuals had problems with drug abuse, compared with 2.9 percent of the general population. Among those who had at least one biological parent who abused drugs, 8.6 percent had their own drug abuse problems, compared with 4.2 percent of those whose biological parents did not have drug abuse issues."

In another study by the US National Library of Medicine National Institutes of Health, *Substance Use Disorders and Adoption: Findings from a National Sample* by

Gihyun Yoon et al, it was found that that there was a linkage "between being adopted and having a propensity to SUD [Substance Use Disorders] years later in adulthood." The strongest linkage was a genetic one with one parent suffering from SUD ("or perhaps related genes such as impulsivity favoring a genetic propensity for SUD in their offspring") and the poor style of parenting. But there the linkage was found, too, with adopted children with "adoptive families with social characteristics better than families at large, including higher education and higher socioeconomic status." The children in difficult circumstances were more at risk for substance abuse but the study concluded, "Whatever the cause, being adopted should be recognized as a risk factor to SUD."

David drank for 32 years. He got sober at the age of 45. And has stayed sober since. There's a saying though, "What do you get when you get a drunk horse thief sober?" (Answer: A horse thief.)

David's problems—particularly the overwhelming feelings of disconnect—remained. And no matter how hard he tried, he couldn't fix himself and it seemed he could never quite fit in—even in the place that welcomed him and helped him get sober. For example, David had problems with the AA slogans—sayings that are popular in the 12-step programs and serve as mini-lessons that can fortify one's new way of living (sober). They range from adages such as "Keep It Simple" to "You're No Longer Alone" to "Let Go and Let God."

David gives an example of "One Day at a Time," which directs the individual to only focus on *here* and *now*. David says, "The reality is that the trauma left a big part of me really stuck in the past, as if it was actually happening." Another slogan that didn't resonate was, "We are only as sick as our secrets." For those of us with traumatic experiences, such as being a relinquished child, keeping secrets about our reality and our feelings can be essential to survival growing up. "Thus, to hear such slogans sounds very shaming. Yes, it is healthy for those of us who have shame-based secrets to release them, but only in a safe, supported context where we feel safe to do it."

For David, it was a combination of things: finding the right 12-step groups (specifically, agnostic groups, where David felt most at home), finding the right mental health professionals, or talking to dear friends with whom he could process things. Feeling safe was crucial to allow David, "to be real and find reality, mine and a greater reality."

* * * * *

Unlike alcoholism or a propensity for seizures—which David suffered from as well—shame is a silent, sneaky killer. As Maté points out, shame starts even before you can imagine it starting—and when you name it, it is there already, before the words you acquire to describe the feelings that go along with your psychological discomfort.

According to Dr. Allan Schwartz, a licensed clinical social worker and a therapist, in his article "Psychological

Issues Faced By Adopted Children and Adults," for adopted individuals, "Feelings of loss and rejection are often accompanied by a damaged sense of self-esteem." There's a prevalent belief that, "something must be wrong with me for my birth parents to have given me away." Those feelings have nothing to do with how well the adopted child is cared for. In David's case, he was a part of a loving family, yet the uneasy feelings persisted. "Guilt accompanies loss and grief because the adopted individual believes that they are being disloyal to the people who adopted, loved, and raised them. They do not want to hurt or betray their adoptive mother or father," writes Schwartz.

David had a beautiful childhood, fun-filled teenage years, and young adulthood filled with adventure, friends, girlfriends, and objects that were the envy of his peers—boats, cars, party accruements—and he wanted for nothing. Yet, he had developed not only depression—manifesting as his inability to form connections, and later, by trying to foster connections through drinking and becoming a workaholic to deal with the emptiness he felt—his insecurity kept accumulating. On the outside, gregarious and friendly, he was a secretly morose teenager and later a confused adult desperate to get close to people but unable to.

According to Maté, trauma can start even before we emerge from the womb. For example, an alcoholic mother can produce an infant predisposed to alcoholism not because of genetics—there is no gene that determines alcoholism—but because both the alcohol she is drinking *and* the stress she is under will physiologically affect the baby, increasing its propensity for addiction or, say, depression.

Maté says, "We know that the brain develops in interaction with the environment from beginning before birth. Hence, the mother's emotional states and stress hormone level will affect the developing child."

Maté also mentions Robert Sopolski, an American neuroendocrinologist, who believed that we are affected by the environment as soon as we have an environment.

"Shaping into who we become as children, and then adults, begins as early as implantation. As a matter of fact, we already know that the trauma of grandparents is translated into the genetic functioning of their grandchildren so [we can have trauma] even before we're conceived," Maté says. As for difficult pregnancies, a mother-to-be releases stress hormones, which then get fused into the placenta of the infant and have an effect on the child's development. Any woman who's giving up a baby for adoption is almost by definition a stressed woman: she has to give up the baby. There are teenage moms, addicted moms…environment happens even before pregnancy. The infant in the uterus is going to be affected by that.

Then, there's the separation [of a baby] from its mother. People say, "Well, kids can't remember that," but yes, they can—they can't recall it, but they can remember. Recollection is having the capacity to recall something, but the structures that make it possible don't develop until childhood. The emotional imprints happen even in utero, the last trimester maybe, and certainly after birth; those are imprinted in body so most of the people who have been adopted will live a life with the sense of abandonment.

David's experience with revealing his adoption to friends marked him for life and became a recurrent psychic pain that never stopped hurting, no matter how much he tried to numb it with alcohol or his work. As mentioned, it was there even when he began his recovery in the 12-step program. It was the kind of damage that kept stopping him from growing, or better yet, from becoming whole.

According to Jamie Marich, a counselor, trauma specialist, expressive arts therapist, and EMDR (Eye Movement Desensitization and Reprocessing) trainer who has worked with David in a patient capacity, trauma doesn't have to necessarily manifest itself as PTSD. (PTSD, Post Traumatic Stress Disorder is a mental health condition that's triggered by a terrifying event—either experiencing it or witnessing it.)

Most psychological traumas produce disturbing memories that somehow get stuck. For David, the memory of the event with his friends haunted him his entire life. Marich approaches trauma as "a learning issue as a result of our unhealed wound, and those messages [that a person gets during the event] become scripts through which we operate in the world. The messages in early childhood are especially pervasive because they are often given to us before we really have cognizant understanding of what's going on and what we might call the rational brain, either because the brain is not yet fully developed or because the traumas that happened to us were at the level before language."

* * * * *

The extent of psychic damage can be conveyed even in words we use to describe the disturbing experiences that shape us. For example, David rejects the term "adoptee" because he wasn't *just* taken into another family—he was, firstly, given up on; he was relinquished. David refers to himself as a "relinquishee." But there's actually more to it than being relinquished. Maté says the word "relinquishment" might not be enough to define an experience of a person given up for adoption. "The word he's looking for is actually "abandoned." The focus is on the abandonment experience. David is protecting himself by using that word [relinquishment]. You don't relinquish a human being—you can relinquish a thing: it's got no feelings. What happens to human beings you relinquish? They experience abandonment."

Marich, on the other hand, doesn't mind the word "relinquished" because the word relates to what happened to individuals who were given up. But whatever you'd like to call it, Marich says, "Those traumas tend to stay, and the body at a young age is not able to feel them or assimilate them into their experience, and they remain unhealed at this level that exists really below words or rational understanding. And traumas that get crystalized and get stuck there at an early age, before the age of eight, are especially volatile if they're not healed because they become a part of our personality, our core identity. [They become] the messages we learn about self in the world as a result of those [negative] experiences: *I was given up on.*"

Maté says that David's relinquishment coincides with "the memory of being abandoned by the birth mother." Maté gives an example on how this might manifest in real life of an adult David, "If you're talking to him (David) and say, 'Sorry, I gotta go,' he feels rejected, abandoned. It's got nothing to do with what's happening in the present—it's got to do with the emotional memory so that the emotion comes back but without the recollection [yet David thinks he's] reacting to the present. He's not. It's the past that's being triggered. That's not unique to people with adoption but it's very strong in them because of that early abandonment."

* * * * *

With adoption, traumas keep going: first it's the adoption itself, then for some it might be foster care and furthermore, [abusive] parents. The child develops emotional coping mechanisms that make the job of a [adoptive] parent more difficult, and the parent gets upset and the child is punished. The statistics are scary: people with addiction have a risk of suicide double the average.

David's adoptive parents weren't abusive, but he was an especially sensitive child, and even his parents' encouragement of independence—such as ordering at a fast-food joint—were sometimes overwhelming and distressing. What was "normal" and natural for others, could be perceived as threatening and unusual to David. Feeling watched, scrutinized, feeling as if he was living under a giant microscope...those were constant companions of David, who didn't know how to be in this world.

Mark Coen, founder of the Attachment and Trauma Specialists, an internationally recognized agency specializing in the treatment of youth and adults with attachment-and-trauma-related issues, writes this about adoptees: "They are generally well liked and even popular, but this is because they are chameleons, masters at being able to hide under the radar without anyone knowing who they really are."

David started drinking as a teenager. He drank to feel connected to people, to be able to fit in. Alcohol allowed him to feel "normal." Drunk, he wasn't so tortured because his feelings were numbed; he felt happy, even social.

Schwartz writes, "According to the great psychologist, Eric Erikson, adolescence involves a search for self-identity. While this search is difficult for most teenagers, it presents special problems for adoptees. Assuming they never met their natural parents and family and have no idea of their genetic background, they are left with a gigantic gap in their search to answer the age-old question: 'Who am I?' This was a major struggle for David. He's lived unsure of who he was exactly and how he fit into the world. He knew he was adopted but he didn't know anything about his biological parents—many of the facts surrounding his adoption were concealed from him by his adoptive parents; there were no conversations about it, and despite the love and care he's received, nobody was asking how he *really* felt."

David's identity was so fragmented he spent most of his life searching for what was missing—mainly his *real* identity, one that would encompass not just his actual life, but also his origins.

Schwartz points out that because of the great unknown that is an adopted (relinquished) person's biological origin, there's also the problem of medical issues. Incidentally, it was a medical emergency that spurred David's quest to find his roots and discover what was wrong with him and why he suffered a seizure in his 40s.

During his search for his origins, it turned out that both of his biological parents struggled with substance use. His mother succumbed to alcoholism, dying a terrible, lonely death in an institution. She had no one and no possessions to speak of by the end of her life, which ended tragically at the age of 56—the age David is now, at the time of writing this foreword.

* * * * *

One of the safe places David found outside of 12-step rooms was a therapist's office. Most significantly, he sought a specialist in eye movement desensitization and reprocessing (EMDR Therapy). According to one definition, "EMDR is a form of psychotherapy developed by Francine Shapiro that emphasizes the role of distressing memories in some mental health disorders, particularly Post Traumatic Stress Disorder (PTSD). It is thought that when a traumatic or distressing experience occurs, it may overwhelm normal coping mechanisms. The memory and associated stimuli are inadequately processed and stored in an isolated memory network. EMDR therapy is as effective as cognitive behavioral therapy (CBT) in chronic PTSD."

For David, the EMDR approach allowed him to "feel real and begin to further trust myself and the journey I was on." David's past had a hold of him; it was a force in his life that kept him stuck, but through therapy, he learned that, "this hidden power could no longer hold me back, and that it could not destroy me as I continued to become whole."

But was what happened to David—being given up by his mother—really trauma? Maté says yes. "People think that trauma is bad things that happen, for example the adoption, the abandonment is the trauma, or sexual abuse is the trauma. That's not the trauma. That's what *triggers* the trauma. Trauma actually happens inside the person. The trauma is not the event but the impact the event has on a person: inside the individual, inside the child—they can't respond to the situation the way they need to. When somebody is abused or abandoned, they need to express those emotions connected to that and have those emotions understood and the respond to them. If the caregiving adults are able to really get the child's emotions, have them fully express these emotions and deal with the emotions, there's no trauma. The trauma consists of shutting down your reactions, therefore becoming disconnected from your body and your emotions—that's what the trauma is. The trauma is disconnection. That's the good news. Because if the trauma was what happened at birth or when you were a child, it's over. [For David] he would need to connect with himself. There's the emotional experience of trauma and there's the story attached to it. Trauma can be healed because, if the trauma is that disconnect, then it can be healed."

David wasn't convinced he had indeed suffered trauma. It was Jamie Marich who became David's therapist and who "validated my suspicions that what happened to me could be viewed as traumatic and healed with EMDR." This therapy, David says, was only an incremental part of the journey, not the turning point. It's what he needed at the time to sustain the courage and energy to deal with life and its realities, as well as the people around him who cared about him.

Through EMDR, the therapist and David targeted David's driving negative belief that there was something wrong with him. It was through allowing himself to see what held him back (the feeling of not belonging) that let David to conjure an ultimate occurrence needed in healing: he faced his fears. He says, "After the end of the entire experience, which was cathartic and helpful in allowing me to connect many of the emotional, physical, and spiritual dots, a major, genuine shift in my core beliefs occurred. Although these connections helped me to arrive at several new beliefs that resonated in both my head and my heart, I was ultimately able to declare with genuineness: "I am more than a victim, a survivor, or a 'rescue,'…I am whole."

Marich says, "Part of feeling whole especially for somebody who feels they're living a double life is feeling like they no longer have to live a double life, that this is who I am. 'Whole' means different parts of my experience are integrated together—for instance a lot of survivors of trauma feel disconnected from their body. But through doing some work they may be able to link that body and mind experience. That's what part of being whole can mean. As it relates to David, being able to embrace 'I am whole' means that there's really nothing left to hide. There's no shame that I have to live with anymore."

* * * * *

This is a story of David, but it is also a universal story of shame and psychic pain; it a is story of a man who was so broken he couldn't put himself together. It is a story of a man who drank to cope with his feelings or, alternatively, to be able to numb them. It is also a story of self-discovery. It is a story of hope.

Today, David is 56 years old. He is a happy, independent addiction consultant involved in substance use disorder treatment and recovery management. He has family and friends who love him and to whom he feels connected. Yes, there are areas where David still strives to evolve further—for example, he remains diligent about fostering the human connections that he has already, and he attends to them as if they were fragile flowers requiring constant maintenance. He also pursues the connections that have been lost—his biological relatives who are still alive: half-siblings—and he continues to learn about his family of origin and absorbs that knowledge to further complete the puzzle of his past. He is rigorous about adhering to his reality and how it informs his life. He is sober, not only in the sense of addiction, but he also has a sober outlook on life—he doesn't shy away from reality. Indeed he considers *Reality* to be his higher power, a force that guides him and keeps him grounded. It is that feeling of reality and being authentic that lets him cultivate deep, meaningful bonds with people.

Although his discoveries might seem personal, they are universal: we've all felt displaced, lost; we've all felt despair at some point. Many of us don't have a good idea what it means to live a meaningful life. We've lost people to indifference and fear, and we've hidden away like wounded animals. The good news is that, although we might be wounded, there are ways to heal ourselves. And David is the kind of man who wants to share his story with the world because he believes it will help others to get to the point where he is now; it might help them see how they too might be able to get out of the rut of self-doubt and mental torture. It might aid their healing. He believes that others can also learn to foster connections on a deeper level, get out of hiding, find the truth, and work through despair, apathy and uncertainty.

Dr. Robert M. Sapolski in his book, *Why Zebras Don't Get Ulcers*, writes, "If I had to define a major depression in a single sentence, I would describe it as a 'genetic/neurochemical disorder requiring a strong environmental trigger whose characteristic manifestation is an inability to appreciate sunsets.'"

And although he is still learning about himself—as all human beings do—today, David does it with courage; he does it in a safe space of *Reality*. He considers himself whole. Today, David is the kind of man who appreciates sunsets.

—Jowita Bydlowska, author of *Drunk Mom*, a memoir

Prologue

Who are you?
What would you say? Think about it.
Maybe you'd list where you live, where you come from,
who your parents are, who your friends are, what you
do for a living, how many children you have, if you believe in God…so many answers to describe what makes
you *you*.

It shouldn't seem that complicated, really, because
you would know many of the answers—it's your life
and you've been there to witness most of it. Most of us
should be able to answer the question with what facts
we have, the evidence. Everybody has ties that keep
them close to other people, to the world—and the world
reflects who they are, too.

Except that the answer to "Who are you?" can be
more complicated than what the evidence provides.

It was—it *is*— more complicated for me. The facts
weren't always accurate; some weren't even facts; they
were lies; the evidence was tainted. I didn't feel *real*—it
was as if I was not quite here, often completely detached
from the world around me.

But later, there was new evidence that changed my
perception of everything.

And once I knew more about who I was, I started to become more real.

It's a process and it's a beautiful one—seeing yourself evolving, connecting to the world in the way that I never dreamed would be possible.

* * * * *

There's always a moment when something in an addict's life shatters. It's a point of no return. You will never be the same. For me, that moment was the moment I learned about shame.

What is shame? "A painful feeling of humiliation or distress caused by the consciousness of wrong or foolish behavior," according to one definition.

I didn't do anything shameful, but I revealed something to the world and the world reacted in the way that made me feel ashamed.

I revealed something that made me immediately separate from those around me. It severed the ties I thought I had; it shattered the trust. And once I became aware of the betrayal and abandonment that happened to me, I felt all these other components of shame: distress, humiliation, foolishness.

Shame became one constant emotion—more powerful than love. Shame was more powerful than reason.

I met Shame for the first time at the age of six, and it haunted me for most of my life. After that, I found it everywhere: in my later childhood, in my high school years, when dating, when working a high-pressure job, when not working. It was as if I was always sitting under a giant microscope of the world. Being watched, scrutinized, judged.

I tried to make myself invisible.

But the microscope lens was trained to see all my faults.

Shame found me; entrapped me. It was larger than me. It was an entity in itself. No longer just "shame" but a monster: Shame.

* * * * *

I even found Shame in the rooms of 12-step fellowships—the same places that had also saved my life. But it didn't save me from Shame. In fact, it had made the Shame bigger, stronger. It doubled the Shame.

I couldn't pray.

"You'll get it one day. Let go and let God, pray harder," the people in the fellowship said.

I couldn't. Actually, no, that's a lie—I prayed every morning, in the shower. I prayed for the real prayer to appear to me.

In sobriety, I prayed like that for seven years. Seven years of Shame like a tumor growing and obscuring the happiness I could faintly feel was possible—but I felt it too faintly, far too deeply inside me; I wasn't sure it was really there.

There was already so much wrong with me, I felt—I was a relinquished baby, a forlorn teenager, a messed-up adult, an alcoholic—and the fellowship was telling me that there was even more wrong with me.

How was I ever to feel safe? How will I be saved?

"Tell me more about God, tell me more about how to get to God?" I stopped people in the meetings and they would look at me with pity. I knew what they were looking at. They were looking at someone who was going to relapse. Because he wasn't *getting* it.

"You'll be saved when you find God," they said. It was crazy-making: you'll get it but only if you...*get* it?

There's no worse feeling in the world than knowing you're not getting the idea that everybody else is getting.

Many people—myself included—in 12-step programs, say that they were born without an instruction manual on how to live.

I had no instruction manual on how to be in life. Or how to be in recovery.

I got down on my knees and prayed, prayed, prayed, and I felt Shame, Shame, Shame.

I kept not finding God. And they kept telling me if I don't *get* God, I will get drunk.

I knew: If I get drunk, I will die. And I kept thinking: *I still don't even know who I am.*

It seemed like the worst cop-out to die before finding out who I was.

* * * * *

Today, years later, as an addictions professional, with a nice chunk of sobriety, I know that you absolutely cannot and should not shame someone with trauma. You must not murder them with Shame. Most addicts have been traumatized. Most have had something shatter in their lives that broke them in so many places that only a drink or a drug was able to glue them back together, temporarily.

I was traumatized. I was broken.

* * * * *

In the movie *Men in Black*, there's a scene where Will Smith's character, J, realizes for the first time that humans are not the only intelligent beings in the universe. His partner, K, played by Tommy Lee Jones, says, "Fifteen-hundred years ago, everybody knew that the Earth was the center of the universe. Five-hundred years ago, everybody knew that the Earth was flat. And fifteen minutes ago, you knew that humans were alone on this planet. Imagine what you'll know tomorrow."

Tomorrow is a possibility. A possibility that includes reality—that of me being a sober alcoholic who is most likely to stay sober. No God is involved in this process—my sobriety doesn't depend on God. It depends on tomorrow materializing itself and on how I will deal with it. It depends on reality.

And reality is that tomorrow, I might learn more about where I come from, more about who I am.

The uncertainty of life is scary, but I've come to terms with it. Every day is profound; the possibility of beauty and joy are always there. Every day I am a new man.

And every day is a new reality, and I stay as close to it as possible.

– David B. Bohl

The Box

There was once a box. Inside this box, there was something that existed and didn't exist at the same time.

It existed in the way that I knew what it was—I saw it; I put it in the box—but it also didn't exist because I put it in the box to not think of its existence. If I never opened the box, I wouldn't have to be confronted with it; and out of sight out of mind, right?

The thing in the box had nothing to do with my reality. That's a lie: it had *everything* to do with it. I just couldn't deal with any of it.

A problem? Perhaps, but we'll get to that later.

For now there was a box with a secret inside of it: an answer to where I came from and what made me avoid who I was. It was all so complicated, difficult, confusing. I needed things *not* to be confusing. There were things that were confusing enough. I needed things to be—at least at the time—sweet and simple. And nothing was sweeter or simpler than Jack Daniels—it was sweeter than my reality, less complicated, a joy to be with, really.

* * * * *

Speaking of boxes, do you know about the Schrödinger's Cat experiment? In this experiment, a cat is to be placed in a box along with poison and a Geiger counter—an instrument used for measuring ionizing radiation—and some radioactive material. When the Geiger counter detects the decay of the radioactive material, it'll trigger the mechanism that will smash the bottle of poison, and the cat will die.

This tongue-in-cheek experiment was designed by Erwin Schrödinger, a Nobel Prize-winning Austrian physicist, to challenge one principle of quantum mechanics that states a particle exists in all states at once—until it is observed. This principle, called superposition, claims that since we don't know the state of the object, it can be in *any* state until observed. In the Schrödinger's Cat example, the radioactive material might or might not decay, and the cat is both alive and dead until the box is opened.

The superimposition theory of things being in two states at once reflects a radical way of looking at reality that led to a theory called "Many Worlds," or what is known in popular culture as "Parallel Universes." Everything that can possibly happen does happen to you here and to you in another universe. And there's an infinite number of parallel universes. You die, you don't die, you live, you were never born, there was a house on the lake, there never was a house on the lake...

There's an infinite number of possible realities.

Schrödinger meant to poke fun at the theory of superposition with his ridiculous experiment (for the record, the actual experiment has never been carried out—animal cruelty was not the point), but the physicists didn't get the joke. Until this day, the magical cat is both alive and dead; you can believe in dubious or not-so-dubious science that, like religion, belongs to the most fanatical people.

* * * * *

My box was not an experiment in quantum mechanics, although the mental equations I'd performed around ignoring and alternatively obsessing over its existence were more complex than any quantum mechanics formula you could write out on a blackboard.

A thing cannot both be and not be. Can it?

Yes, it can. In fact, *I* am and was that thing. I am the real proof of Parallel Universes existing, of things being and not being at the same time.

I am a paradox: a man who wasn't even born until he was in his mid-40s.

I am a man who was freer than most and who was imprisoned at the same time.

I was a man with a box with answers and a man who refused to open the box. A man with many answers to questions he had asked, but who still questioned the answers.

I was also a man who couldn't leave his basement, and I was also a sailor who raced with the wind.

A wise man. But also an alcoholic.

A social butterfly—a guy who made fun happen— but also a recluse, a relinquishee, a nobody.

Today, I am all of those things but I'm also more: I'm evolving, and I'm no longer at war with myself. And I understand my reality. *My* reality, that is my Higher Power. *My* Reality.

This is a story of Parallel Universes and secret boxes and a secret man who became known, who found himself within many universes to finally become one with himself.

Freedom

Imagine the wind in your face so strong that it feels as if it could cut right through you, but instead of letting it do that, you align with it.

Your hands and body attune to it, too, the wind, and then the water, too—and the force of the wind and the water push you as you steer the boat, razor fast, through the sun-sparkled waves, to the finish line.

Fast.

Faster.

Duck, move, stretch, hike, pivot—hands pulling and trailing ropes, carbon-fiber sails above your head, water splashing in your face, your mate's back strained in front of you, elbows flying at your face, and your breathing so heavy you fear you might hyperventilate; and you move, move, your body; not just your body—your body is the boat's ballast and gravity now, keep going, push, pull, advance with the wind, keep pushing.

The adrenaline pumps hard, from your heart right to your head; the adrenaline is what feeds you, and the more it courses through you, the more you want of it; and the turns are sharp, dangerous—every gesture could mean a loss or a win. You calculate all of this as you move your body and propel the scow through the water; you become a human machine.

No mistakes so far. So you keep going, your body aligned with speed at all times, propelling you; your crew reading the wind and the water and your movements to make it to the finish—you have to finish, get ahead of everyone. You live on adrenaline—you even call yourself an "adrenaline junkie"—and there's nothing faster now than your calculations and your heartbeat: only the speed and the sail and the water ahead and the finish line. The scows around you are like in a video game, just obstacles to avoid and to get around, nothing else.

You get around them, you avoid; you keep going, because you will win this race because you are the wind and the wind is you, and the adrenaline is like rock'n'roll music, loud and hard in your ears, pumping you to make it to the end.

And now, finally, all the other scows behind you; it's smooth sailing as they say, except it's not smooth. It's still aggressive, it's fast, more precious now that the win is so close, but you feel in sync with all going on around you—you split the water wide open till you're past the finish line and everything else is behind you, even the wind.

You've won!

Afterwards, it's the familiar faces, the same faces that just an hour ago battled and conquered the wind with you, and the hands that hauled the ropes to orchestrate the race are slapping you on the back, everyone slightly out of breath, but breathing in and out, breathing the triumph of the won race. The reward…the reward doesn't really matter, because the real reward is you and everyone else around you slapping you on the back, and the first drink in your hand—that is the real reward: the hiss of the liquid down your throat, the calm after the storm that you've partaken in. Your body is no longer aligned with the wind—it is now aligned with the drink. This is a magic moment. And for this magic moment, you know this is where you should be, this is life, nothing else matters, only the drink and the water behind you and the wind is now calm.

The storm is coming but it's not the real storm—you're way ahead of the storm, so let's celebrate, here's another drink and more familiar faces, everyone laughing, "Man, we did it, we showed them, here's another drink, congratulations."

That was freedom.

That was no freedom.

The Lake

A lake is a beautiful thing: with days ending in reflections like crystals shimmering on the surface of it as the sun sets, and with mornings full of freshness and promise.

At night, a lake is an extension of the sky. Millions of stars above as you lie down, facing the sky, the waves lapping gently against the side of the boat. You are cocooned, lulled to an incredible sense of peace.

Growing up by a lake alters you—the natural, good energy of it stays in you forever, and you can never quite leave it behind. It's a siren voice that calls you over and over to come back and immerse yourself again.

It's safe here, the voice says, *it's home; it's love.*

Unlike an ocean, a lake is quieter, more reliable; the water is sweet and the calm is its prerogative. Not always, of course—there are windy days and rainy days as everywhere else, but even during those, a lake doesn't betray you the way an ocean does with its capricious storms or tsunamis.

On a lake, the calmness makes it seem as if every day is the same, but then, wonderfully, every day is different. Nature ensures that seasons pass and the water freezes in the winter and wakes up in the spring. The trees grow taller, the lake kids become grownups.

You know those primal smells of childhood that go straight to your heart, that bring on nostalgia, gentleness tinted with sadness for things past?

For me that smell is fresh lake water—it goes straight to my heart, and I'm simultaneously here and now, and there and then.

The water is the only pure space where I've experienced something akin to spirituality.

The one place I feel at home.

For me that specific water was—and is—Lake Beulah.

It's my past, my childhood, and all the happy moments of that time. I still go back to Lake Beulah, but I no longer live by some of its rules—I mean, by the lifestyle that I've left behind, the fast boats, the fast drinkers.

I can't do that anymore. But it feels safe now, again, because I am okay in this world.

In the past, at Lake Beulah, during the summer, in the day, there was a beach I visited as child, before my dad built a family vacation home, but the beach is now long gone, having been developed into single-family homes.

The lake is a harmony of sounds: of grownups and children talking and laughing, and music filling the air around you. Closer to the shore, swimmers splash about, and in the distance the lake is alive with sails, unfurling like wings.

In the evening, the sun sets in every color imaginable: purples and pinks and yellows and myriad shades of blue, and you can walk out onto a wooden pier to bid another beautiful day farewell. The smell and sound of water and distant voices bring an unmatched peace and tranquility as you stand there and look into the sky, look at all this wonder swaddling you in total awe.

At night there is that specific, muffled night laughter, and clink of bottles, and I think of the times when I was a teenager and we would take our boats out onto the water and tie them together, joking and teasing each other—we were full of youthful energy and the conviction that we were special, invincible the way all teenagers are convinced of that.

The grownups would stay at their lake houses, on patios, drinking too, laughing just as much as the kids on boats. There was magic in the air—it felt as if the summer would never end, and it was hard not to think that we'd live forever buzzed on all this beauty and alcohol.

* * * * *

As I write this now, it's winter. I look out the window and there are a few slim, leafless trees with branches like lace; behind the trees, there's a plain of blinding white.

In the winter, the lake becomes a giant skating rink, the trees around it like the ones I'm looking at, leafless but not foreboding. The trees are more like an enchanted fence around the frozen body of water.

Back when I was a boy, I related to that frozen lake. On the hard surface, there was ice, restraint, the distance of coldness, hardness… but underneath the hardness? Life and soul. So much of both: fish and plants—the lake wasn't dead nor asleep; it was just adapting to the season around it the same way I've learned to adapt from an early age.

Parallel Universes

My mother had dark hair and olive skin. She was beautiful, the sort of a woman who stood out in the crowd, almost movie star-like with her strong, yet feminine, features. Her smile was a smile that knew things—a smile of former sadness that eventually metamorphosed into contentment, happiness even.

* * * * *

My mother was a red-headed beauty from the University of Wisconsin. She had freckles and blue eyes like me. A smile full of sparks, girly mischief. Later it was a crooked, tragic smile. She was a deadly fire compared to my adoptive mother's stillness like calm water.

* * * * *

The former mother was the mother who held me on her lap, seven days after I was born; the latter mother gave birth to me, then relinquished me. I went from being unwanted to being doted on; the banished baby, then the most-fussed-about baby in Greenfield, Wisconsin.

* * * * *

Joan, my adoptive mother, was meant to parent—in fact, one word that comes to mind when thinking of her is "motherly." She was the quintessential caretaker: protective, proud of her house and her children. We were her life. This is not to say she was just a little housewife—in fact, the opposite; Joan was a matriarch, a lioness who made sure we felt loved and didn't want for anything.

You would think that she learned those things somewhere, that she grew up in the world where family values came first.

She did learn. But I don't think the lessons were about family values being important. The lessons were, perhaps, the opposite of that. I believe her life was difficult, and so she had to figure out how to make our lives easy to break that pattern. As a young woman she probably felt she had only herself to rely on, at least when it came to her father, who wasn't always there for her and whose anger and bad habits might've disturbed her, made her become protective of what held meaning for her: us, her own family.

Joan's parents were Polish immigrants who struggled to make it in the new country, and there was never any money because there were eight children and the dad who maybe drank a little too much. Joan was close to her mother and protective of her, but she was barely out of childhood before she had to take on responsibilities of a grownup, become a caretaker of her family of seven brothers and sisters.

In a way, her siblings were her children too— my mother delivered most of them in her mother's bedroom. She told horror stories: one was about one of her brothers being born and how she came to, exhausted, to see the entire bedroom covered in blood, the ceiling, her girly body soaked in it, too.

But that was her lot, and Joan took care of things. She became a perfectionist. She became hyper-vigilant: surveyed her environment for danger all the time—back then to escape the mad father and later, when we were her family, to protect us.

She grew up in constant fear, in a survivor mode—the unpredictability of a violent father would do that to you.

There was one night she talked about. Her father picking her up from a babysitting job and driving home, before deciding to stop at a bar.

"You can't tell Mom," he said after he left the bar.

"But I can't lie to her," she said.

"We'll see about that," the father said and drove on. He drove until he reached a hill, and then he let the car climb the hill, hands on the wheel, his mouth determined. Joan, only 15, sitting in total terror, paralyzed. *What was going to happen? Why was he doing this?* There was no way to guess what *was* going to happen—you couldn't predict anything with someone who was so unpredictable.

When he reached the hill, the father stopped the car, killed the engine.

I imagine there was a long silence, the terror thick like smoke hanging in the air, my mother suffocating in it. Maybe she thought about what her life could be like if it was a happy girl's life, carefree—maybe she pictured her girlfriends wrapping their hair in rollers before bed, complaining of their rooms being too hot, writing down boys' names in their journals…normal girl stuff.

But here *she* was, not like them, the little big Joan in the middle of the night with a man who scared her, but who was also her father, her throat and her guts constricting in fear.

Was she going to tell on him? He asked her again and smirked as he turned the engine back on, directed the car downhill and took off his hands off the wheel. The car started rolling down, faster and faster as it gained traction.

Was she going to tell on him?!

She didn't want to die. She told nothing.

* * * * *

By the time Joan turned 15, she had a nervous breakdown. She never said much about it, but I know it was laced with shame and grieving over the childhood and innocence she barely got to taste. The nervous breakdown was internal—she still functioned, went through the motions until she turned 20, got married, and ran away from the nightmare of her childhood.

* * * * *

The life with us was a respite, a chance to redo all the evil she had experienced. She was roughed up by her childhood, but she didn't give up. She was one of those people who is determined to do the exact opposite of what they know, if only because anything is better than just relying on the teachings of their own past. Where there was fear in her life as a child, she made sure she provided safety for us. If there was uncertainty in her life, she never let on.

The house, too, reflected the opposite of what she grew up with. No blood on the ceiling, no cramped bedrooms, no piles of dishes or laundry no one had time to do because there were all the babies to attend to. Our house was spectacularly clean and organized. It was a haven of safety and love and comfort.

My mother was strong: she never succumbed to her circumstances before, and she wasn't about to when she had us. Her strength came from the most vulnerable place and she triumphed over it. With us, she showed herself and the world that it was possible to overcome the darkness; fill the world around you with light; reinvent yourself in whatever way you desired.

* * * * *

Years later, I saw a social worker's report that was meant to determine if my adoptive parents were suitable as parents.

The social worker described my mother as very nervous.

My mother, holding me in her lap, saying over and over, a wonder in her eyes, "Who would give up such a beautiful boy? If she only knew what a beautiful child he was she would never give him up…"

Is she questioning her parenting skills? Is she second-guessing her decision? That's what the social worker wondered about in the report.

My father was noted as a calming influence.

I was allowed to stay; we became a family. My mother's old life was getting erased by the new life she was about to create, that she was going to make perfect.

And it was perfect for a while.

* * * * *

"Who's my biological mother?" I asked my adoptive mother as a child.

"She was a red-headed cheerleader from the University of Wisconsin. Your father was captain of the football team," my adoptive mother said.

She made it all up, she claimed later when I confronted her.

Except it didn't seem like she made it up. Whether it was an incredible coincidence for her lie to align with reality or if she was hiding what she knew from the beginning, I won't know, but when I finally found out who my biological mother was, it turned out she was indeed a red-headed student from the University of Wisconsin, although not a cheerleader.

She had blue eyes like me, pretty mouth, but in most photographs I have of her, the smile is lopsided, never fully there. Her name was Karen. "Karen Ann

Bender"on my birth certificate. (I sometimes refer to her innocently and forgivingly as "Young Miss Bender.")

My father wasn't captain of a football team—he was a linebacker and fullback in football, though, and played basketball and ran track; he was an athlete, an upperclassman who swept Karen off her feet. I will never know what kind of romance they had, but before it ended—tragically—I imagine it as the kind of sweet American love story you sometimes see in movies.

I imagine them catching each other's eye somewhere on the football field, my mother so bright, a teenager with hair like fire, the kind of girl who stood out in a lineup of girls with her 100-watt smile—the smile she had before things broke inside her. She must've blinded my father with that smile, that red hair demanding attention. He probably thought he had just seen some kind of an angel and he knew that the angel must become his.

And he must've blinded her, too, although he was no angel in her life—more like a malevolent force, although not because he was evil, but because he was a kid, weak and influenced by his family, who essentially taught him to *unlove* his fiery angel.

The reason he had to *unlove* her was me; at that time still just a question mark in her womb, although as the question mark was becoming more of an exclamation mark—more of a certainty—some decisions had to be made.

"What are we going to do about this?" my mother, possibly pointing to her belly, possibly said to my father.

She must've been so scared. She came from a Lutheran family, a good family. This was 1950s. There were only a few solutions and one of them a backroom abortion, which was not a solution at all.

"I can't be the father," I imagine him saying when he came back from talking to his family.

"But you are the father!"

"It must be somebody else's."

"Somebody else's? Impossible."

Did her blue eyes well up with tears? They probably did—how could you be stoic in the face of such betrayal? How could he not be the father?

He was the father. Unless I am the second-coming of Jesus—and trust me, I'm not—my mother was a virgin before she met my father.

When it all sank in, did she wipe her tears, was she mute with indignation, or did she rage at him? Or was she so ashamed that she simply walked away? She must've felt so alone. Abandoned. Betrayed. Shamed.

I understand what it's like to be abandoned—she abandoned me later, of course, but then maybe it was my biological father who abandoned both of us, who left her with very few or no choices at all. Or maybe it was his family. Or religion that would've deemed my mother a sinner. Or the society that was embarrassed by unwed mothers and hid them away like lepers.

In a way, Karen was used to abandonment, or at least she was used to not attaching herself to people, so maybe my father's betrayal didn't even surprise her that much after all. Maybe by then, she was enough of a realist to not fight too hard to try to convince him—she knew she wouldn't be able to. People around her made decisions for her, and he was just like them. Her family moved a lot, and she never stayed in one place long enough to form meaningful friendships. Her parents were drinkers; there was some turmoil, though she seemed close to her father.

But despite her unstable childhood, Karen was an industrious person, too—she saved up for and owned her first car at 16, which was a feat back then, especially for a girl. She worked in a restaurant; she had many goals—she was in college before I happened.

Still, despite trying to be strong, she was quite fragile—like my adoptive mother, she too had a nervous breakdown in her first year of college when she was failing zoology, which she found a difficult subject. She felt unwell and underwent several medical tests, but there was nothing wrong with her physically.

And then, finally, with me in her belly, she was getting broken for good and in more ways than one—her entire life was crumbling, my father's paternity unconfirmed, denied by him—he was the father but he was not the father.

Alone, and with the baby on the way, Karen's goals faded away. She dropped out of school. She had to disappear—at least for now. Her family knew it would ruin her life to have a child out of wedlock—those were the times. Karen had to go away, and away she went to a so-called Maternity Farm, a home for unwed mothers in Oconomowoc, Wisconsin, where I was born on August 12, 1960. Karen–or "Young Miss Bender"—was 20 years old.

I don't know if she held "Baby Boy Bender" (me) in her arms before I was taken away, or if she had relinquished me before I was even born, in her mind, and allowed me to be taken away before she could lay her eyes on me. Whichever it was, I can't imagine it would've been an easy parting—one not tinted with guilt and shame and tragedy. There's longing, some kind of a deep sadness in her blue eyes in the pictures I have of her—sometimes I wonder if she never really let me go.

When she finally got back from the home for unwed mothers, things at home were different, too. Her own mother had died of a heart attack when she was away— Karen was now motherless and childless.

She didn't go back to college. She became a stewardess—the perfect job for someone who has never quite landed—and then she got married and became a housewife. But she was way too far gone into her darkness by then. She was a housewife with too many gin and tonics, stashed bottles, secret sips all throughout the day.

She was tragic. My arrival and the circumstances of my arrival changed Karen top to bottom—she was never the same 100-watt-smile girl, unless, of course, you count the blitzed grin of a drunk, which is who she became.

Where my adoptive mother thrived from having me, this mother withered from not having me.

Yes, she gave me up, but I have a lot of compassion for her now, and having gone through my own darkness, I know that her alcoholism was probably just the way to deal with her reality; it allowed her not to face it—she could still be in the world, but she no longer really had to be there at all. She didn't have to think of Baby Boy Bender, and if she did, well, he was just some abstract thing. Who could really remember those things in the half-blackout that the rest of her life became?

She tried settling down, but how do you settle down if nothing in your life ever seemed sure? Settling down was a reality she wasn't familiar with. In her lifetime, she gave birth to five more children—four from her first marriage (one died within a month). She drank her way out of the first marriage, became pregnant, and married another alcoholic so that her last child—the fifth one— would not be born out of wedlock the way I was.

* * * * *

At one point in my life, I lived two miles away from the home for unwed mothers where my story began. I found this out later. It was a great coincidence, perhaps something almost like fate? There were all kinds of co-incidences—my biological mother being the red-headed coed my adoptive mother made up, for example—and there were all kinds of connections, but none of it meant that I've ever gotten closure.

And that's okay. There's no such thing as closure. It's a trendy term, a meaningless term, because you can't ever dissect your past from yourself, wrap it up in a piece of paper, tie it with a bow and burn it and pretend it didn't exist, a thing that you're cured from. I tried to treat my relinquishment and adoption as a sep-aratist movement, just as society had suggested, but that is an absurd concept. We're not machines; we cannot get our parts separated, engines replaced—we've got to fix what we've been dealt, make it all work somehow.

There are always scars from wounds we receive. But that's okay, too—that's what makes us, too, those scars. The only thing you can get from learning about your past, from finding out things like: *Oh, I lived two miles away from where I was born*, is that you finally have some kind of context of who you are.

There are always going to be questions, things I won't know. I will never know the intense pain she felt as she hemorrhaged and lost a lot of blood two days after I was born. I will never know my adoptive moth-er's fearful joy as she maybe held me in her arms for the first time. I will never know my biological mother's grief—or relief—as she placed me in some strange social worker's hands.

* * * * *

Two Parallel Universes, two realities. I was marked for life, destined by my circumstances to have my perception warped from the get-go. But a baby is a baby—it doesn't know the weight it carries with itself when it changes mothers, it has no sense of history or the future. A baby has no idea that his life is good or bad. Eat, sleep, eat, sleep—the least complicated time in human life is unknown to us.

My name is David, but I am also "Baby Boy Bender," born in the home for unwed mothers. Who is Baby Boy Bender? How can you be two people at once? But he's not a person; he was erased, transformed into me. Perhaps he's a ghost.

I was unique because of my circumstances, but in pictures I cried and laughed just like any other baby. Ghosts don't show up in pictures—they awaken later, in our memories, when we finally figure out what has been haunting us all this time.

A New Life

I believe I was loved from the start. I never experienced neglect and my arrival was long awaited. My new home felt like home from the beginning. I was the first child in the family. My sister was born two years later and five years after that, my brother came into our lives.

We were the perfect American family—happy kids and loving parents. In pictures we look like a postcard. Everything matched—our smiles, the sun reflecting in our eyes, the freckles…

No. The freckles were only mine. And the sun, as much as I loved it, was poison to my skin where my family could bathe in it without a care in the world.

I can't remember when I became aware of not looking like them, like my loving, olive-skinned folks, but once I noticed it, it was hard to ignore it. Occasionally, it would occur to me I was like a stranger inside my own home. I was never made to feel like an outsider, but I felt it acutely.

Other than that, I had everything that a boy could want: toys, a bicycle, and in the summer, at our lake home, a little sailboat and a motorboat (a dingy). In the winter a Ski-doo to whip across the lake after it froze over. My parents were successful entrepreneurs who ran their own single-family home construction business.

Our primary home was in the suburbs: West Allis, Wisconsin. Where we lived, in a blue-collar neighborhood, my family and I were often called "rich" by neighbors and friends. The way they said it always sounded dirty—it made me feel guilty even though it was not my fault. But envy is poison, and it poisoned me in that way as a child.

* * * * *

Even in terms of childhood homes, I didn't stray away from the theme of my life's double realities. My primary home didn't feel much like home, or at least not like the place where I felt entirely comfortable. But, thankfully, there was the second reality, specifically the second home on the lake—the one where I felt safe and where I fit in.

The people who came to the lake were wealthy, different from the people in the suburbs. I admired these people—it seemed to me that they were not only nicer, but also more accepting of me.

Perhaps the lack of financial troubles had something to do with that—once you take the envy away, there's room for sympathy and seeing each other as equals.

I understood later in life that people in the suburbs weren't bad people, and that they couldn't help how they felt and how they treated us in turn, but as a child, I could only differentiate between nice and not nice, and the people of the lake came out on top. To me, they seemed more intelligent, more driven, and more ethical. They came from the North Shore and suburbs of Chicago and had lives I had no access to—this made them attractive, mysterious. Even their clothes were different from what I saw at home—they wore pressed shirts, khakis.

* * * * *

Although there were times when I felt I didn't belong at the lake, I almost never felt comfortable in town. It probably didn't help that I never spent summers there the way all of my school friends did. I didn't develop the kind of close friendships that get cemented by summer adventures. Not only that, we started going away to the lake every weekend—my school friends I spent time with almost exclusively within the walls of the school and during an occasional walk home together or a short play date.

During the week, I didn't see my lake friends, so parts of my childhood were spent longing for close friendships that couldn't form under such restricted conditions.

With time, my parents became so invested in the lake they would pull us out right before Memorial Day, meaning we'd miss a week and a half of school, including year-end activities and celebrations. In addition, they wouldn't bring us back for the start of school the last week of August, instead keeping us by the water until after Labor Day.

* * * * *

In the summer, I experienced all the wonders of friendships, and I finally made connections I'd so longed for. There were maybe ten or twelve lake kids who were my age. After some trial and error, I made two or three close friends and had maybe five more acquaintances.

I even met a girl I fell in love with there. We met when I was eight years old, and today she is my wife, and we still spend all of our free time at her summer house: on the same lake, which gives me the same feeling when I look out the window, a happy nostalgia for things that passed. Except today, there's calmness to that nostalgia and fondness I feel when I think about all the good times I've had with the friends who are still in my life.

These were the friendships that mattered to me more than any desperate connections I tried to make back home. And they seemed even more precious after what happened back home when I told my school friends about being adopted.

I'm Not Like Them

Children don't know. They don't know what will impress other children, and they all try to fit in and pick things in their lives that they think make them "cool," unique, different than their peers, but in a way that's socially acceptable. Whether it's a toy that nobody else has or a holiday that sounds impressive, they will try to show off and stamp their "coolness" on the playground, something that will make other children look at them in awe.

I was like any other kid, and I too wanted to show others that I wasn't just a little freckled boy who came from a "rich" family, which didn't seem to impress anyone but only brought on envy.

I couldn't impress with toys or holidays specifically for that reason—I didn't want to "rub in" my difference in that way. So I picked something that in my eyes was a great thing to brag about. I picked my difference of being adopted. To me, that was a neat thing—my parents didn't hide it. Just the opposite–they made me understand that it was a normal thing, albeit not common. To me, it was the difference that would show others I was in some way special, but not bad-special. I wanted others to feel about me the same way my parents felt about me:

I was a child who was so wanted he was hand-picked like a precious jewel to make others happy and proud. I was proud of my background then, of my difference. Why would I believe otherwise?

* * * * *

This is the first clear memory of my childhood: I was walking home from school with two of my friends. I was six, full of eager stories. There was always excitement in exchanging fascinating facts—we were all so young, everything seemed amazing and new. I too had a fascinating fact to share—better, I thought, than anything I'd heard from them, from any of my friends. With some nonchalance—just wait and hear how amazing I am!—I mentioned that I was adopted.

They stopped, we all stopped, their expressions confused, eyes scanning my face.

I expected a reaction. Surely they would be as cool with this as my family was; surely they would think that is something to brag about a little. Why would I believe otherwise?

But it was otherwise. It was so otherwise that almost as soon as I said it, I knew it had been a mistake to reveal myself in that way.

My two friends laughed. Uneasily, but there was cruelty in that laughter. Their little faces twisted disbelief and something like horror.

"You were what?"

"Adopted," I said, albeit now less sure that this was the right thing to tell them.

They couldn't believe it. They said they didn't believe it. They called me a liar.

"I'm not a liar! It's true!" But as I shouted it, I realized that I shouldn't be defending this so hard, that maybe this amazing thing wasn't amazing at all. I felt my body grow hot and cold, then hot again—this time with Shame.

"Liar!"

"I am not a liar."

Why would I lie about this? In retrospect I wonder if their "liar" was partly so they wouldn't have to change their mind about me—their insult, "liar," was almost as if they were offering me a way out. I would admit to being a liar and they would be relieved that I wasn't adopted. Being adopted was turning out not to be so amazing; it was turning out to be a dirty secret I should've kept to myself.

But maybe there was a way to still make this into a cool thing? I was desperate. I wanted someone to confirm what I believed just minutes ago—that being adopted was great, that it wasn't a lie.

I wanted to feel again that it was a good thing, that there was no reason to feel ashamed of it. Yet Shame already had started seeping in like poisonous gas. I ignored it for now. I insisted on bringing my friends over to my house so that my story could be confirmed. If they saw how my parents thought of my adoption, they could maybe wipe that disbelief and that look of horror off of their faces.

We walked toward my house in tense silence. Something was wrong. But I wasn't lying. I was cool. It was cool. I had to explain. It had to be explained.

The side door slammed behind us—it still echoes in my mind, that sound, the metallic clang that severed my innocence.

My mother, sweet and strong as always, welcomed us cheerfully. Her darling boy's friends were coming to visit. I wonder if by looking at us, she could tell there was some gravity to that visit.

"I told them I was adopted," I said to my mother. "Am I adopted?" I said, hearing doubt creeping into my voice, but not because I didn't believe I was adopted—after all, I knew, and it wasn't a big deal at all—but because I wanted my mother to straighten everything out, say what an amazing thing that was.

"Yes, Dave was adopted. He's our son," she said something like that, something along those lines. She was confirming my revelation. She seemed relaxed, happy about it. She loved me.

But my friends' faces didn't show what her face showed—their faces only showed more confusion, although under the kind but watchful stare of my mother, they possibly stuttered something about how neat…and we could all tell that they were lying.

I knew then.

It wasn't neat or cool. Or amazing. Or good.

It was bad.

I was bad.

I could tell then for sure that my confession was backfiring. It only demonstrated that I wasn't like them. I could tell that instead of being impressed, they were feeling sorry for me.

Immediately, I understood that to be adopted meant that somebody—my red-headed coed mother—didn't want me. That I had been discarded, relinquished. And that my parents perhaps took pity on me, and that perhaps they loved me only because I was a poor abandoned boy.

In the social worker's report my mother was noted as saying, *"Why would anyone give up such a darling boy? Why would he not be wanted?"* Her lovely wonder alarmed the social worker—it showed her that perhaps my mother was overwhelmed with the task she was taking on.

I didn't know about the report until later, but my mother's wonder was always there and now I could feel it changing: its positive glow become something ugly, something to be ashamed of.

My friends were pitying me and they were embarrassed for me. It was like showing them a deformed part of my body or something and saying, "Look how fantastic this thing is! I am a monster!"

If I was a monster, but insisted on that being a great thing, they would think I was delusional, which is what I felt right in that moment. They thought I was a fool or that I was fooled into thinking this was all a good thing.

It was a breaking point for me. My Shame was suddenly present, too obvious to ignore; it was big and triumphant and it wouldn't leave for most of my life.

* * * * *

If you were to look at pictures of me from that time, you'd notice a significant progression. In the pictures "Before the Reveal," I am a happy, cheerful kid—full of life and promise, albeit always shy and a little unsure. In the pictures "After the Reveal," I am contemplative, closed-in and mistrustful-looking.

My biological mother's betrayal was reflected in my friends' faces so clearly. Their expressions said: *You were unfortunate, a lucky bastard somebody out there wanted. You were not wanted, you were taken because there was no one who would take you, not even your own mother!*

Is that who I was? Yes, that was who I was.

I believed it. I believed their horror. I was fed a lie all those years and my friends' reaction showed me what the truth was.

My parents tried their best, I know that. But sometimes I felt that the world created for me was a little bit of a fantasy. I wondered if this fantasy was because, perhaps, my parents' love for me stemmed from mercy? I wondered if I was a mistake because I had been relinquished. I worried that I should be eliciting pity; that I was maybe a charity case—those were only my impressions, but they came to mind. And who wants to be pitied? Who wants to be a charity case?

Nobody, that's who. All the toys, all the privileges, all the love and care, were because my parents were making up for the mistake that my life was. My parents were trying to correct the mistake.

I panicked.

I realized then that perhaps everyone in my town thought of me this way. I was indeed right in believing I was under some special scrutiny.

Before it seemed like delusion I needed to talk myself out of, but now it was confirmed that it wasn't a delusion, that the eyes I had perceived as judging were, in fact, judging.

My friends left probably talking about "poor Dave" on their way home where they were wanted from the beginning, where no one thought of giving them up because they were rightfully in the world. They were no mistake. I was a mistake. I was cursed.

I believed everyone else had already named it, what I sensed, and they called it Pity.

Little Baby Boy Bender wasn't even named by the woman who was supposed to be my mother, a safe person who was supposed to love me unconditionally, but who couldn't, wouldn't. Who wasn't safe. Who was so unsafe I had to be taken away from her.

* * * * *

It was different at the lake—my relinquishee status didn't really bother people or at least I was never made aware of it in the way that made me feel ashamed.

Yet, despite the lake world's acceptance, I remained a careful, distanced child—the distance growing since my revelation—and I struggled with feeling fully connected even on the lake. There was suddenly an unmistakable distance. I never felt watched or scrutinized with disgust there, the way I felt it at home. I was just a kid, allowed to be, no big deal, welcomed to play with other kids like I was just like them. But now I knew I was *not* like them.

There is a photograph of me sitting in a little boat looking away from the camera. No one takes photographs of children like that anymore, but before, when you couldn't edit sadness, when film simply captured the reality, the photographs show the truth. I am slumped in that boat, and my stare is a stare of someone knowing the truth that hurts.

A small boy, a lovely boy—just like any small boy is lovely before he becomes a complicated grownup—with resigned shoulders, carrying the weight of that truth.

As a father now, I look at that picture and I know what it represents, and I think about that boy as if he were my own, and I want to help him, but how do you help yourself in the past when you're in your future? I could only use that picture as a clue to what I am today. The little boy with Shame consuming him like an illness that you can't ever recover from—or that you learn to understand but only after years of trials and errors.

In subsequent pictures, there's certain melancholy in my eyes. When I look at those pictures, what I see is a visible shift between innocence and loss of it document-ed and clear, setting me up for a life of detachment. I was given up on. And now, I gave up on myself. Adaptation became a coping mechanism I needed to employ constantly; this world was not mine to be in. An adoptee adapting—lucky me, I knew the perfect way to be. I could pretend. And why not? The world was a joke.

* * * * *

I learned many years later that the experience of being taken away from a biological mother can be severely traumatic to an infant. Loss and abandonment are common among reliquishees; many suffer from things like Reactive Attachment Disorders (RAD) or even Post Traumatic Stress Disorder. Psychologist Nancy Verrier talks about something called the "primal wound," an emotional, psychological, and spiritual injury that occurs at separation. Some adoptees have referred to this condition as "cellular," as in the kind of pain that you feel in your very cells. How do you heal from that? It's like some kind of a cancer of the mind.

I didn't know any of this as a child or even later, as an adult. But I knew the entire time that something was missing—whatever a human core was, wherever it was; it seemed, it was not in me. Maybe it was my biological mother who unwittingly took it away from me as they took me from her.

And was I looking for my biological mother in everyone? Did I distrust everyone because she had abandoned me? Was my distrust confirmed at the age of six?

As awful as it was, it seemed to me like the first truth—those boys' reactions and my suspicion that there was something wrong with me. It all aligned with my suspicions. I was unwanted. Despite all the evidence—a safe upbringing—everything in my life was built on a lie.

Shy

I don't know if it was that early sense of Shame, or maybe the fussing attention of my family I've always felt—sometimes more like a burden, heavy on my little boy's resigned shoulders—but I became a very shy child.

I hid behind my mother's skirt whenever anybody visited, my eyes wide and terrified and a freckled nose peeking out curiously, but also pleading, silently: *please don't look at me.*

It was a problem, the shyness, and my parents didn't understand it. But how could I explain to them that sometimes it felt as if I was being judged by the entire world around me? Maybe it was unreasonable, sure, but so are the monsters under your bed and Santa Claus when you're six.

"Go on, don't be shy, darling. It's just McDonald's," my mother said as I was pushed toward the door of the fast-food chain.

"What are you, an idiot?" said my younger sister. She rolled her eyes, "It's not a big deal!"

Sure. It was not a big deal. Except my heart was pounding so hard in my ears and I felt like a tiny bug under a giant magnifying glass. I had to order some food. There was no way in the world I would be able to do it.

What if I were to just start running? Run and run and run until I would simply disappear somewhere behind the line of the horizon?

Who would run after me? My stupid sister on her short baby legs? Ha.

I could escape; this was a matter of life and death!

"Darling boy," my mother said.

"I can't," I groaned. Did she not see that I would die if I were to walk through the door? How could anyone think this was not the most dangerous, awful thing to ask a child to do? But if it was, why was my little sister able to do things like this and I wasn't? Why was I feeling so totally hopeless?

My sister obviously understood how things worked and I didn't, which is why I remained frozen, my thoughts like scurrying insects unable to sit still for a second so I could figure out the way out of this mess.

"I can't," I wanted to say again, but I was suddenly mute and my body seemed paralyzed. "*Move*," I said to my body but it wouldn't. So now I couldn't run, I couldn't escape.

On top of everything, I knew that my face was getting red—I could feel the heat from the inside, enveloping my entire body. I couldn't understand how my cheeks weren't bursting in flames yet. I hated feeling myself blush—it was essentially like announcing to the entire world how scared I was.

I felt a violent push—but it was only gentle fingers of my mother, merely brushing my shoulder—yet I would still not move forward.

"Come on, Dave." The hand rested on my shoulder. It weighed a hundred pounds.

"Idiot," my sister said.

"Come on, Dave," I wasn't sure if the voice was mine or my mother's.

I moved finally, one foot forward, then the other one.

I was now walking. I couldn't believe it, but I was, indeed, moving forward. Then there was the door. The door as heavy as if it were made out of iron.

I pushed the door with all my strength.

I was now inside.

The cheerful McDonald's yellows and reds vibrated in front of my eyes, the frenzy at the counter seemed somehow hostile, alarming—surely there was something unusual happening there, maybe someone was having a fit?

No, there was nothing, nothing special was happening; this was merely a busy lineup. It's just that I immediately perceived it as dangerous when it wasn't. Those were the sorts of insights I gained later as an adult when I understood that perception is not necessarily reality. But at the time, standing there with wide, terrified eyes, I was in the throes of hell. Without looking, I just knew that every person turned around to look at me, observe me from where they were sitting.

I didn't have to check to see their eyes saying: "*Who is this weird little boy and why is he standing there? Is he some kind of an idiot? Why is he so red?"*

"*I'm sorry,*" I wanted to scream and run out the door, but behind the door were my kind but non-budging mother and my awful little sister. Somewhere, too, buried under all this panic there was reason: *This wasn't a big deal at all.*

I had to overcome my fear or I would disappoint my mother and my little sister would only make fun of me more. I would possibly disappoint all those people who were now staring at me, waiting—I would disappoint the world's magnifying glass under which I was still hesitating, my face on fire.

Move.

Again.

I moved.

Again.

The world stood still and watched. Judged.

It seemed like decades before I reached the counter. In my head I repeated the order and I was genuinely shocked when the words came out of my mouth—I thought I would no longer be able to speak.

I had to wait for the food to appear. How was it that they called it "fast" food if it was taking so long? I was not an impatient boy, but now, under the stare of the world, the wait was excruciating. I tried to shift my body, but it wouldn't budge, then when it did, I moved so ungracefully I almost bumped into someone. I turned to read the menu: *Cheeseburger, Milkshake, French Fries, Apple Pie...*

I re-read the words. One more time. There were five vowels in "Cheeseburger," "Milkshake," had three. I wasn't sure if I was still being watched, but in case I was: *Look! I'm just reading the menu! The menu is extremely interesting! I'm not bothering anyone, please, please stop looking*—I was losing my mind.

Then, finally, the food arrived and I grabbed the paper bag and the tray and walked, stiffly, without looking at anyone—the bravest little boy in the world—toward the iron door that was no longer iron, but was instead light as a feather. I was free! I did it! I didn't die. I passed the test. I wasn't sure what kind of test, but then I looked up and saw love and even a tad of pride in my mother's eyes, and I knew that the test was worth it. I hoped I would never have to repeat it.

My sister smirked, but she too looked a little impressed. It hurt to know how cruel she had been just minutes—was it only minutes?!—ago. I reminded myself that she was only a kid, not even a big kid like me.

The car filled with the smell of food. French fries and burgers, delicious smells that made your mouth water.

I couldn't really smell its deliciousness at first. Or I could, but it only irritated me. My palms sweated. I would have to eat a hundred hamburgers to calm down this anxiety. Instead, I wolfed down the one hamburger I had and I didn't even notice if it tasted good. The panic opened some kind of hole inside me, which the hamburger filled temporarily. Once it settled inside the hole, in my stomach, I was hungry again but also still nauseous from anxiety.

I heard my siblings laugh and tease each other and my mother saying something to me or to them; I couldn't tell.

Slowly, as we drove, the relief washed over me. I was safe again, the hellish red and yellow of McDonald's somewhere far behind us, then, finally, gone.

* * * * *

I wish I could say that that was a one-off. I haven't catalogued all the instances where I felt that shy, but there were many, many times. And it was always as if I just couldn't get *it*. What *it* was, I'm not sure but others got *it*; people in my family, for instance, like my sister — they just knew what to do. The only thing I knew how to do was trying to make myself invisible, which is pretty hard when you're a strapping, red-headed youngster, one of those eye-catching kids.

Or at least I had a feeling of always catching eyes.

Another time that's engraved in my memory is of me in the barber chair where I sat, propped up, about to get my first haircut. Suddenly, I became aware of interrogation lamps trained right on me. *What did they want? Why me? Please go away…*

I wasn't really hallucinating. I was just propped up high on the chair. In reality, nobody was looking except for the barber and my mom. But I felt exposed. Maybe it was my own reflection in the mirror—I was scared to look at that too. My shyness was eating me alive from the inside. I couldn't explain it to myself.

The only explanation I could come up with was that I've felt that way because everyone else could see what I knew and what I tried to hide: I was different from them. Relinquished. Not just different from my dark-haired parents or different from my peers at school who were angry about how "rich" we were, but different in general. Often it felt as if everybody else got an instruction manual that I clearly had not been given. I bet there were things in that instruction manual, such as how to relax in a barber chair, how to sit less stiffly, how to make that come to you naturally.

There were probably entire sections on how to order food from McDonald's, or maybe just one short section that screamed *"Don't worry about it, relax,"* and you could read that and you could actually stop worrying about it and you would relax.

In the barber chair, I felt my face grow hot. As usual. Again. My mother was looking at me, an encouraging smile on her face. It didn't help.

I tried to swallow, but my throat was so dry it seemed to try to close in on itself. I closed my eyes, too. I didn't want to see the world, and I wanted it to stop looking at me. I kept my eyes closed for a while. I had to figure out how to deal with this situation, how to get through this haircut and not just crumble to the ground or start crying or pee myself or all three together.

"Darling," my mother said.

I sat paralyzed, feeling as if I was about to have my head chopped off instead of my soft, reddish curls.

I Hope Someone Out There Will Find Me

As I got older, my sense of Shame and isolation never went away after the event with my school friends. I was less uncomfortable at the lake, but even there I felt a certain degree of detachment—I still never quite belonged despite how accepting the lake people were. I wanted to connect to others so badly, but at the same time, there was some comfort in knowing that I was right all along about my being a fraud.

Experiences shape us. The one with my school friends was traumatic—it shaped me in a way that informed how I saw the world now: a place in which I couldn't trust—really trust—people, where I would never be whole. At that time I didn't have the words for it, but it continued to be obvious to me that I hadn't been given the direction that would show me how to be in the world. How did everybody else know how to be? It was baffling. They knew something that eluded me. Even when I tried to be as present as possible, it was as if there was an invisible wall between me and everybody else.

Sometimes I was so clueless as to where I fit in, I simply missed people trying to reach out to me. For example, I would go around the lake in my little motor-boat looking for something social to do. I was feeling terribly lonely.

I would pass shores where I saw friends and see them watching me, and decide that they wanted nothing to do with me. I don't know what made me decide that, but I felt it deeply in my gut: *They want you to leave them alone, David.*

So I left them alone. I steered my boat away and went around the lake again.

Later, I would hear from the same friends, "What's wrong with you? Are you stuck up? We're friends and you don't have time for us?"

Of course, that's what it must've looked like to them. Yet, I interpreted their staring at me as judgmental; they interpreted my driving away as snobbish. Later I thought of that song, *Boulevard of Broken Dreams*, the lyrics illustrating what that felt like back then.

* * * * *

I sailed alone, but I was always wanted and loved by my family. And yet, it didn't matter. They lied to me, or at least omitted telling me the truth about how shameful it was to be adopted. At that time, their sheltering me from the world's nasty judgment about adoption was a bad thing, something I could be angry about, something I could use to justify my distance.

I didn't want to die, but I didn't want to be noticed. My shyness was stronger than ever, and it seemed that

I was finally finding some comfort in it—or that it simply corresponded better with the feelings of Shame and isolation I was feeling so acutely.

More and more, I was becoming a wallflower, trying to blend in with the background so as not to offend the world with my unwanted presence. There were only a few moments in my life where I remember someone—other than my loving but busy parents—making an effort to *find me*. One was a coach named Jim in the Catholic Youth Organization program who intuitively knew I needed to be found. He coaxed me out even though I couldn't even speak due to my shyness.

As we waited to be chosen by the two baseball captains, I felt that excruciating dread many children are familiar with when playing team games with their peers—the dread of knowing you might be the last kid standing, the last kid to get picked.

I was not a particularly popular boy. I worried I would be the last kid standing. I heard Jim say to one of the captains, "Look at this big kid. He looks pretty strong; he should be on your team." And I got picked right then and there.

I only knew Jim for a few months, but he gave me the feeling I had lost. For that brief period of time, he made me feel truly wanted: I had the right to be here, after all! The feeling didn't last long, but the taste of it was so sweet, it masked all the bitterness of my unhappiness.

I got glimpses of this feeling, again, many times over the years, but it wasn't until I was reborn as an adult that I realized I had every right to be wanted; I had every right to be here.

Pressure

See that kid about to start the car? He's maybe 14, although he looks older. He's a big kid, that's why he looks older. But he's still a kid. I am — was — that kid.

Inside the car, my entire family — a little sister and a baby brother included. A highway unfurling ahead of us. Drive? No big deal.

"What are you doing, Dick? Are you nuts?" My mother's alarmed voice pierced the air as she turned to my father.

He had already made up his mind. He wouldn't argue with her — things were going to happen *his* way. I knew this about him, we all did. My mother was a matriarch, but my father's silent demeanor was more powerful than her protests.

Tension filled the car — it came from my parents arguing, but also from my siblings watching all of it, excited to see how it would end. I liked how impressed and jealous they seemed to be of me, behind the wheel — I, too, was proud of my father's belief in me. It meant that I had done something to deserve this responsibility, even though at the time I couldn't tell what it was exactly. I don't know if he had been drinking, if that was why I was asked to drive. At that time it simply seemed like a thrilling opportunity—albeit a terrifying one too—and I was too excited to worry about his reasons.

I can't say it was a huge surprise that my father would bestow such a demand on me. Sure, it was unusual and sure, I didn't even have a learner's permit, but I was used to doing things that none of my peers were doing yet. Exciting and terrifying things, just like driving before I was legally allowed to drive. But it was all about adaptation! I was good at that, a pro.

Early adaptation was where it was at: I had a boat before any other kids, I shot a rifle early, I was allowed to drive the camping trailer three hours away from home with a bunch of friends when I was barely 16. I was a mini-adult before I became an adult.

Back then, it was as much fun as it could be, even though I could feel something else besides the excitement. A little bit of dread. Or maybe a lot of dread? I couldn't tell if it was a lot—it would only appear once in a while, and then I would try to talk myself out of it instantly. I was given so many wonderful opportunities, why would I sit and dwell on that?

Because it was stressful—sometimes everything seemed like a test. And to that confused boy passing the test meant staving off the world finding out about me-being a fraud.

As for my father, he was kind and loving, but also too quiet. It felt as if I had to guess what he was after when he'd give me new responsibilities. What he was after was teaching me through experience, allowing me to make my own mistakes. At the same time, hearing him insist in the car, "David knows what he's doing" to my mother sounded more like a test, too—but I could only nod: *Yes, I know what I'm doing.* If I didn't know what I was doing, that would mean that my father was wrong about me and that he made a mistake in trusting me. My father didn't make mistakes. I couldn't fail him that way.

* * * * *

My friends thought I was indulged. They thought I was lucky. I thought I was lucky, too, different from my sister and younger brother because they didn't get the same privileges. They were coddled longer and I had no patience for coddling. I was a teenager; I couldn't wait to live life to the fullest.

When I look at the pictures from that time, the expression that prevails is of fake confidence mixed with caution.

Rare smiles.

Unsure smiles.

Sometimes my parents got into arguments over how much my father pushed me to be independent, and my father defended me; he defended my maturity that I myself wasn't so sure of. But I loved him for it, and I loved him for all the trust he put in me.

Still, I wish he'd talk to me more, but he was a quiet guy—his praise was measured and doled out in more responsibilities rather than in words. His manner was always that of someone who lived in the moment, but because it was practical, not because of some strange philosophy—it was a method he applied to make his life uncomplicated. He didn't spend too much time worrying about the past, barely letting us, his family, get to know him.

I knew some things. I knew he had been an altar boy, raised in the faith of the Catholic Church until the day of his confirmation when he realized he didn't believe in God.

He probably had no idea that this declaration would also mean he would, in a way, become motherless—more specifically that his own mother would disown him over what he no longer believed. She herself was already in trouble with the Catholic Church, being a divorcee.

It didn't stop her from marrying again—a man who adopted my father's sister, but not my father. My father became an orphan who had parents.

Years later, he would build a house for his mother and his sister. He never complained about what had happened to him as a child. He had moved on from that; building the house for his aging mother was the right thing to do. Practical. Many others would have their revenge, but he had only mercy and kindness.

When he was old, I tried pushing him for more information, but all he said was, "I came from nothing; I was the first in my family with a college degree."

That was all he wanted to share.

He never said anything about the heart with the word "Alice" tattooed on his left upper arm. Who was Alice? What had happened to Alice? He was a mystery. He was too silent. It was that silence that broke me even more, eventually.

Fun

My teenage years were wild, unsupervised, full of doubt and swagger at the same time. I was a king. I was a pariah. Everything was happening according to the theme of my life: parallels. I was a guy at war with himself.

But there was one way to suspend the war and it was through magic, specifically alcohol—it made me explode in joy in the way I never knew was possible.

Drunk, I liked myself, my own enemy.

I liked *them*. My friends. I was drinking with them. My friends or whoever those people were—well, with alcohol coursing through my veins like blood, everybody was a friend.

I was making connections, felt ties that seemed deeper and more meaningful than anything I'd ever experienced. With this magic, alcohol, in my system, it was as if I was reborn or maybe repaired—the disconnect that haunted my childhood disappeared and I would finally feel at home…anywhere, everywhere.

I couldn't believe it.

It was so easy to access the world now and all you had to do was drink!

It was truly something magical—the answer to all of the questions and doubts I had ever had. The war could be won.

I was…happy. For the first time in my life, I was truly happy.

And to increase my happiness, I drank more. I drank in bars with friends; I drank on boats with friends. I drank Friday nights during football games in high school. We would get blasted and sit in the stands and watch the game.

I found drugs, too. So many drugs. Wonderful, terrible things. I smoked pot, hash; I ate speed, pharmaceutical-grade methamphetamine, Dexedrine. I could do ten pills at once, one night. I could smoke a bag of weed. I could drink like a fish. I was hungry, insatiable. Life was mine to consume—I was on top of things.

I was incredibly lonely.

I was on top of things.

I was living in a delusion.

Occasionally, it was like finding myself awake in the middle of a dream, screaming to break through the film of the dream and not being able to pierce it. The false magic of alcohol would even reveal itself a little. I had glimpses of reason; it was all so superficial, not entirely true. The friendly pats on the back and wild jokes and confessions—all of that was just an image in a funhouse mirror, not entirely authentic.

But was there any other alternative? No. I was screaming for connections but I also knew this: I've walled myself in with my drugs, my booze. Nobody can get through.

I didn't want anybody to get through.

I wanted somebody to get through…anybody.

* * * * *

I upped my game. I started dealing things I was consuming: marijuana, black hash, Dexedrine…The loneliest guy was becoming Mr. Popular. Everyone wanted to be my friend. I made mad money. It was madness. There were no consequences.

I was on my own. Two weeks of parties—my parents bought a vacation house in Florida—and a crazed, free lifestyle that every 16-year-old dreams about. I *was* living a teenage dream.

My customized van was legendary around town, with benches and a refrigerator in the back, an 8-track tape player, and a CB radio. I played 8-track tapes on my stereo with huge black speakers. I had a toolbox full of drug paraphernalia under the driver's seat. How would you not want to be my friend?

Then there were the 6:00 a.m. parties I threw deep in the woods where kids from my school could buy a plastic cup of beer for a buck. A quarter barrel of beer. The kids lining up with shiny eyes, girls giggling behind their hands, and pushing each other as they stood in the lineup. Boys posturing like they were tough. Some were.

But the king of the keg was the toughest one of all with his blazing red hair, big strong body, and nonchalance to match his size.

There were more drinks during breaks. The same kid king tried to make sense out of words that fell out of teachers' mouths, but it was mostly just gibberish, nonsense. The whole school was a joke; it was pointless to sit there and burp golden clouds of beer quietly.

By noon, I was done and I'd skip, drunk and not giving a damn.

Occasionally, the vice principal would call me into his office, but my honesty—"I just skipped"—would undo him every time. He'd ask me not to do it again; I would do it again.

So?

My locker was full of drugs. More than a hundred branded, yellow, plastic disks that were used to cover the top of a quarter barrel tapper to keep it clean. I wondered what would happen if my locker got raided—I imagined shocked faces, gasps as all the madness would spill out in a cloud of powder, sweaty beer scent, and the thick, dark smell of hash. What would be the consequences?

Oh, who cared anyway? It was a funny thing to think about. It would never happen. It never happened.

* * * * *

My secret loneliness haunted me, but you'd think that I would develop a better idea about how to get closer to people eventually, because how could you not, with all those friends around. My house was full of them when I threw my parties; there were people asking me for drugs, for booze, for a laugh, for a drive. I strutted through the parking lot and sometimes I was so high—literally, figuratively—that I felt like I was a rock star.

But the closer to people I got, the further I got.

Once I made myself vulnerable with a girlfriend and I clung to her desperately, like I was a lost child. I was a lost child. But she wasn't looking for me; she didn't want a lost child. Not that I was childish—I just needed her in that overwhelming way that is sometimes dictated by the first rush of infatuation. I didn't know how to control it. I was an out-of-control guy.

I was going to convince her she needed me like that, too. I wanted to be with her all the time—she was the first person to whom I opened up to a little more than was comfortable. She held my heart in her hands. She was my salvation.

She dropped my heart. Her hair sparkled in the light. Her eyes big and bright. Like sun setting on the lake.

I was clueless.

You don't cling to people to connect to them. You give them space so that they can breathe, see you from a distance instead of getting crowded by your demanding presence.

"David, I love you, but I've got other things going on," Madeleine said.

She was breaking up with me. The sun was now gone. In the night everything disappears, but once you get used to the darkness, you can make things out. Somewhere in that darkness, in the Parallel Universe, alcohol winked at me, like a star—the alcohol would never do that to me, break up with me. My True Love. Not Madeleine.

I would be with it again. And then my belly would become warm; there would be that weakness in my legs that was pleasant. My True Love was singing to me, filling me with her song, making me forget about the girl whatever her name was—I couldn't remember suddenly—I was somewhere else entirely. I was in a place where I knew the truth. The only truth: I was unwanted. The girl didn't want me. My suspicions were confirmed once again—I had no idea how to be with people. I was a fraud. I was not who I seem to be outwardly. I was no boyfriend.

* * * * *

It was better to continue not trusting anyone, not let anybody get too close to me. And, sure, there were more opportunities with girls, but I was done with that for now—I only wanted to be with my True Love. I could always count on her.

There were girls taking their bras off, girls being forward, girls wanting to get to know me—it didn't matter.

"Whatever, okay, great. Do you want another beer?"

The girl's forehead crinkling. Was I blind? What was wrong with me?

There was nothing wrong with me and I wasn't blind. I didn't care. Or I cared, but not about them, about their breasts.

I just wanted to drink. And get high. I didn't need anybody else—not them, no one—to see the real me.

No. I desperately wanted everybody to see the real me.

No. I didn't.

I did.

Parallel Universes.

I got up to get another beer. A girl pulled the shirt over her head. Or maybe she left. Or maybe she wasn't even there in the first place. It didn't matter.

I drank and drank and drank...

Disappointing

I t was around that time when I learned two monumental lessons of my life. The first one was not to get caught.

Because I got caught. In a local bar, a tavern. There was one on every corner.

It was a school night and we were making magic at some rickety table, a whole bunch of us, friends who drank.

There was some commotion at the door, everyone looked up. A troubling blur came slowly into focus: Cops!

My fake I.D. didn't match my face. I looked older than my peers, but perhaps there was still something in my features, a certain innocence and soft skin that wouldn't fool sharper eyes. And that night, some eyes didn't get fooled.

"It's a school night."

I shrugged as the cop stared at me. I wondered if I should tell him a joke, make this situation a little lighter, but I decided against it in the end. *Yeah, it's a school night, so why are you here? Ha. Ha. Ha.*

I decided to say nothing. I knew I was in trouble.

I was taken to the police station with my buddies, who also got busted.

Their parents showed up right away, and after a short while, it was just me in the cell. I sat and waited and waited—there was nothing else to do. I was still buzzing from my interrupted night, but the alcohol wasn't enough of a buffer to protect me from the feelings that were now flooding in. How could I have been so careless? Who gets caught like that? Only a total idiot, obviously. I need to be more careful next time. Go somewhere else. Get a better fake I.D. I was having such an amazing time. *This is only a small glitch*, I kept thinking.

But the longer I sat there, the more sober I was becoming and the larger the glitch seemed. Where was my father? I knew that he wasn't doing anything that late at night—what was taking him so long?

I waited. And waited.

Monumental life lesson number two—he was teaching it to me by his absence. His absence said more than any words could. He was making me wait. It was more upsetting than if he were to show up right away and punch me in the head.

I hated the uncertainty and I hated the certainty of having realized what he was doing.

When he finally did show up, I was completely sober, or at least I felt sober in all senses of the word. I felt sober and somber.

I apologized. Again and again.

He said nothing.

I followed him to the car. He still wasn't talking to me. Nothing.

I knew he was a man of few words, but this was maddening. I wanted him to shout at me.

Hit me.

Anything but this!

We sat in the car. He didn't turn the engine on.

You know how they say that silence can be sometimes deafening? This was a deafening silence. Heavy, loaded silence where there was no escape into the words because I knew that it didn't matter if I talked. He had to talk first. I had to wait for him to say something—my opening my mouth and pleading would possibly only make things worse. My father had a saying: *He who speaks first, loses.*

It's not that I didn't want to lose—I had lost already—but I couldn't say anything out of respect for him; it wasn't my place to say anything first after the many *Sorrys* that fell out of my mouth already. So I sat and waited and then finally he said: "David, I'm very disappointed in you."

He spoke first, sure, but it was I who lost. Immediately, I echoed what he said, in my head: in *you.*

It was as if my world ended right then and there.

I know it might not sound so terrible what he had said, but because he spoke so rarely and he was genuinely a loving, caring guy, his words after that heavy silence carried a judgment so great that I crumbled under it.

It wasn't, "David, I am very disappointed in your behavior," but, "David, I am very disappointed in *you.*"

It was *me* he was judging. Only me. It killed me. He called me out on what I had already suspected about myself most of my life: that I was different, alien…disappointing.

I couldn't talk to him. I knew it would be pointless to ask him how to make up for my mistake, how to be in this world full of temptation and the magical elixir of alcohol, how not to disappoint him.

There were so many things I wanted to say and couldn't. There was no constructive criticism and no actual punishment. Just that one sentence that was my real sentence—it wounded me mortally.

It was pure Shame, the thing that was my kryptonite, my Achilles heel.

My father's silence silenced me.

I didn't need to be shamed. We both knew I was smart and maybe I was hanging out with the wrong people. Maybe there was something that was troubling me that we could talk about, maybe we could talk about my disconnect, my unconscious desire to create chaos in my life.

Those are the things he could've asked me, but he didn't ask me anything. He had already made up his mind about me. I was disappointing. In those moments, my loving father was a judge and I felt humiliation so enormous I wanted to crawl under my seat and never come out.

We drove home eventually and I went to sleep mortified, bleeding from the invisible wound I had just been given.

It left a scar that didn't heal for a long time.

* * * * *

Humiliation and Shame are great motivators—I never disappointed my father in that way again, but for weeks after that night, I couldn't even look him in the eye. And it felt as if I was walking on the proverbial eggshells all the time.

I wanted to disappear—I wanted to be free of the Shame that wouldn't leave me alone. I felt it grow bigger and bigger again, swallowing me again. Whatever fake courage I've gained from drinking was now completely gone in those sober days, and I kept spiraling into the darkness of my own beliefs about my non-belonging.

Evidence

If you asked me then if I knew I was an alcoholic, I would think it a ridiculous accusation. You cannot be an alcoholic and still be a teenager—it makes no sense. Alcoholics were a specific breed of people, like a friend's drunk uncle, the butcher's wife everyone always whispered about. The gym teacher who always smelled, faintly, of something fermenting quietly in his pores. The guy behind a dumpster or the very old guys you saw at the tavern who could no longer remember their own names.

A kid cannot be an alcoholic; it's an outrageous thing to even suggest that. I was just wild. Just having fun. Who doesn't get caught with a fake I.D. at 16? Come on.

I got caught with a fake I.D.—and so what? My father got disappointed. My father was disappointing, too, making me wait that long back then. There was such quiet brutality in that lesson.

In any case, hear that *click* and *tssst*?

That would be me opening another beer. It was New Year's Eve. My high-school years were about to end with a bang. Literally.

Still, at this point, I was away from that particular climax; I wasn't even at the New Year's Eve party yet. Just driving. Soon, I would be at the party.

The car skidded a tad on the road but it was nothing—I laughed. Boring. Ha ha ha. I was invincible.

The beer felt warm in my belly—whatever happens, happens, but there will be no landing in a ditch. I took a big sip. More warmth. My reflexes were fine. I saw everything clearly. My body was happily pumping alcohol, heart to head and back. Tonight was going to be amazing; best night of the year. We would be making true magic, drink to get drunk. Simple. Except tonight it was going to be even better. There was going to be more alcohol and more drugs; everyone would laugh just a little louder.

I had an idea to convince some kids to run out naked into the snow. That would be hilarious. I had lots of ideas. *This will be an unforgettable night*, I kept thinking. I gunned the engine.

Soon, I was inside and the party was in full swing. It was lights and laughter and people saying what a hilarious joke I just told—*what joke?*—and I laughed because yes, I was hilarious, and there were people upstairs doing some speed so I ran up the stairs, someone said, "Watch it," and a drink tumbled down in golden bubbles and it splashed against a wall. It didn't matter, it was funny and stupid and I wasn't going to "watch it." *You watch it*, I said or maybe just thought it. I shouted for whomever I was running after to wait—it seemed I was on my way somewhere, but where? I couldn't remember, but there were two of my closest friends, Mike and Bob—or was it Kevin?—and they were talking about some kids outside in the snow doing something crazy—running around naked, really? They really were doing it?

I couldn't understand if they were or if they were just talking about some kids trying to do it—did it matter? Idiots. No.

Someone handed me a beer and I drank it in one gulp to clear my head, and then Peter and Dan were gone but who was this guy that I was talking to now? I didn't think I'd met him before. Was he from our school?

But god, the girls. Inside, the girls wore tube tops that drove us boys wild with lust. They were all Cheryl Ladd from *Charlie's Angels*. The air smelled of their perfume—cheap and sweet like candy. Their eyes were big, huge eyelashes and blue eye shadow. The girls looked so beautiful–all of them. Like fairies or snow-flakes...I said that to someone and she giggled; there were bubbles above her head. Maybe I was just talking to a glass of something—*more Champagne?!* Someone said or maybe I said it but I poured more—of course, more Champagne.

I popped another pill. The picture came into focus.

There were lots of people at this party. I knew some of them or maybe I didn't know anybody—almost immediately the focus started getting blurry again.

I popped another pill; then another *click* and *tssst*. Focus, unfocus.

I was standing with my best friends again, whatever their names were; one was saying something about getting in our cars and going to make doughnuts in the icy parking lot of the near-by mall. Crazy. There was no way I was going to do that—it sounded like a great idea!

"Sure, man, sure," I said and someone said I was *the man*—I was!

There was clinking of glasses and then more hisses of beer cans opening, and more laughter and then it was time. Everyone started clapping and hooting, "Happy New Year!"

What year was it? 1977—the year of leisure suits and rock'n'roll music: Led Zeppelin, Pink Floyd, The Who, David Bowie, Fleetwood Mac (Stevie Nicks was to die for), Neil Young, Aerosmith, Lynyrd Skynyrd, ZZ Top.

I loved the wild music of Babe Ruth and the super-hot Janita Haan, too. It rocked my soul to the core; it made me feel almost as invincible as booze did.

1977…I hated *Saturday Night Fever*—yet I owned a pair of black leather platform boots. But I loved *Saturday Night Live*. *Star Wars* had just come out and made very little impression on me.

I wore a bandana as a statement of rebellion.

I smoked Old Gold cigarettes at 75 cents per pack, and gasoline cost 75 cents per gallon.

Microwave ovens had only recently been invented and were truly high-tech appliances to marvel at.

Watergate and Women's Lib were still political conversations. Billie Jean King vs. sexist Bobby Riggs in the tennis Battle of the Sexes.

"Happy New Year! Happy New Year!" Somebody was kissing me and I was kissing somebody back; everyone was kissing and shouting even more and there was confetti, sparkles everywhere. I had what felt like a mild heart attack, and then I had a headache, but I drank the rest of whatever I was drinking and the headache was gone like that—a miracle! And I popped another pill...or two.

The night was turning into a zigzag; the walls seemed to be made out of electricity. I could no longer stand on the floor—it was as if I was surfing on a big, unpredictable wave. I tried to hold onto things, but I could only try to get hold of the wall or rather glue myself to the wall, which remained rubbery and unreliable. It was time to go home before everything disappeared for good inside the zigzag.

I moved slowly, cautiously.

Outside, the sharp winter air smacked me in the face. It was probably more effective than the speed I've been taking all night long, standing in the cold. But what fun is standing in the cold? I didn't know where my jacket was. Did I have a jacket with me? It didn't matter.

I breathed in the air and it filled my lungs with crispness. It was not enough to make the world stop moving, again, but I stood outside for a few more moments trying to clear my head, trying to undo the zigzag and turn it into a straight line. But the zigzag had now turned into a pinhole and everything around me was black.

This was ridiculous. Why was the world doing this to me?

There were shouts in the distance, more laughter. The party was still going strong. But the pinhole wasn't getting any bigger.

It was time to go. *Soon, you'll be home, warm in your bed*, I told myself.

I climbed inside my van, turned on the heat.

The driveway was a long snaking line that I tried to watch with one eye open to make it fit through the pinhole. I drove slowly, followed the snaking line.

I opened my other eye; the pinhole became two pinholes, two snaking lines now. I closed one eye—BAM— the van shook violently, an earthquake to my right side.

I was suddenly sober, only for a brief second, only to realize that something happened. I swerved, half-doughnutted onto the main road, unintentionally, but I somehow managed to straighten out the van. Hopefully I was on the right side. I laughed to myself and stepped on the gas.

My house was dark, quiet. Outside, the snowy silence calmed and made everything a little dreamlike. It took a moment for the key to fit into the hole. Damned key. I would have to get a new key—there was something wrong with this one. I could barely make it work. It's happened before with the same key. Other times, the key worked just fine, like when I left for school in the morning.

Maybe it was my eyes. Maybe I needed glasses. It was hard to see in the dark; it was not the key's fault.

Quietly, I opened the back door.

I tiptoed through the house like a ballerina. It was a feat since the house wavered and tilted but I managed to make it to my room where I too tilted right into bed. There was a bang in my head, a sound of laughter fading away, shouts, *Happy New Year!*

Then silence, darkness. The perfect darkness, the perfect silence.

* * * * *

"What happened to the front of your car, David?"

My father was sitting on the edge my bed.

It hurt to open my eyes, but I had to pretend I was fine so I opened them as wide as I could: *See? I'm fine!*

"The front of my car?" I whispered.

"What happened?"

"It was so icy. And foggy," I croaked. "I started to skid. I smashed into a pole."

My father's eyes, watchful but trusting. A sigh, "Okay, David. I'm glad you're okay. We'll get it fixed. Was the party good?"

"It was good. I left early. Everyone was getting too drunk."

"Glad you left then."

"Yeah, me too," I thought, and darkness fell over

me again except this time I was here to witness it; I was sober and awake.

I had hit something.

What if that something was a person? The image of a car popped out at me; snapped into intense focus and I knew then: I had hit a car. But what if a person had been getting into that car or getting out of that car? I shuddered.

I couldn't think about it. It was stupid to think about what ifs.

What if the owner of the car found out who—?

No. It was stupid to think about that, too. Everything was fine.

* * * * *

"*Tssst*," the first beer can of the year opened a day later, once the hangover was long gone like the bad dream of *what ifs*.

The laughter was subdued—everyone still recovering from the epic New Year's Eve party—but the beers were flowing and the music was playing loudly.

I took a big swig. My belly started to slowly fill with pleasure. I was tuning in and out of the many conversations around me.

"I called the cops," Ron said.

"Whoever did it was an idiot," another friend said.

"Did what?" I said. But in that moment, I knew even before they told me. Ron's car had gotten crashed into on the night of the New Year's Eve party. He went to the police. The police were looking for the idiot who did it.

"Probably some loser drunk," I said, making sure my voice didn't shake.

I was telling the truth—it had been some loser drunk. It was me. I didn't say that part. I felt my body grow hot and cold the way it always did when anxiety struck particularly hard.

I took a big swig of my beer.

It was time to move on to Yukon Jack. The beer wasn't doing it.

I stayed silent for the rest of the conversation with the exception of a few sympathetic grunts and head-shakes that would show how upset I, too, was on my friend's behalf.

How would I tell him about the car? I couldn't possibly tell him.

I was a coward.

I had to tell him.

I couldn't tell him. I would go to jail, maybe. I would disappoint my father, again.

The rest of the night was a blur, but not because I drank too much. I couldn't seem to see past my Shame or something; there was noise in my head, thoughts crowding, yelling accusations at me in my own voice.

I left and went home and slept a troubled sleep, tossing and turning.

I worried about the cops. They were looking. Looking for me.

* * * * *

Three days later, I went to talk to Ron. I told him. I said, "My windshield…the night; it was foggy. I couldn't see very well. I wasn't feeling great. I was sorry. I didn't mean to drive away. I didn't mean to—"

"David. I thought we were friends. What are you doing?"

"We are friends!"

"You wait three days to tell me this? When you knew? What kind of friend does that?"

I'm a piece of shit, I thought to myself, but out loud I just kept saying, "Sorry, sorry, sorry…"

My friend didn't say it, but his eyes did. He was disappointed in me. I was disappointing, to my father and now to my friend. Not just to this friend—to that whole group of people with whom I drank just two nights ago, faking my shock and disbelief at the hit-and-run.

There was no recovering from this. I had lied to everyone. No matter what my motivations were, my confession now would only look like I was trying to save my ass before the cops found me. And I *was* doing that—but not just that. I was also trying to salvage the friendship, but it was becoming obvious that trying was pointless. There was no friendship to salvage.

I deserved to be humiliated. There was something wrong with me. I wanted to say this: *There's something wrong with me*, but the words wouldn't come. I didn't know what to say.

"David."

"I'm sorry, man," I said again.

* * * * *

We were never friends after that.

The cars got fixed — mine, his.

I didn't get fixed; I was now more damaged than before. Shame triumphed again and it laughed in my face as I tried to run away from it. It cornered me every time, breathing its foul breath, saying it knew everything about me because it was me. Shame was me. I was it.

Still Not Here

The movie *Animal House* with the infamous John Belushi didn't come out until 1978, causing a cultural phenomenon for those of us on college campuses. Marquette University banned it and never showed it at their theater. It didn't matter—the whole place was *Animal House* in real life.

I was taken aback by the amount of puking, fighting, drinking (!) and general running amok of my peers. Not that I was above getting hammered—it was, in fact, my favorite thing to do on my own. But the overall behavior of the kids at my new university was ridiculous, childish. I had gotten that childish recklessness out of my system in high school—my unusual freedom probably had a lot to do with that.

Often, I was overwhelmed by my anger. I couldn't stand these people. One more idiot throwing up in the hallway and I was outta there. I should get outta here anyway—what was a non-believer doing in a Jesuit college in the first place?

A non-believer did what his atheist father told him to do. The college was close to home. Despite all the permissiveness, there must've been something in me that alarmed my father enough not to let me get too far away.

Years later, as a parent, I understood that, as impermeable children can be sometimes, they give off insecurities and fears they don't talk about but are obvious to a father. And protective instincts kick in. Maybe that was the reason why my father insisted on Marquette. I wanted to go to the University of Wisconsin. My father went there. Years later, I found out my birth father had gone there. Parallel Universes?

If I had to characterize that period in my life, it was a time of more adaptation. I adapted to my father's wishes, to the new place where God was an authority bigger than science.

In high school, I had been trying to mimic the kids in flannel shirts and blue jeans and their hatred of rich people, despite being the opposite. And at the lake I had to adapt too—flannel shirts off, khaki pants on.

By the time I got to college, I was conforming to every environment I needed to fit into. I didn't have skills to trust myself. For all the disgust I felt toward the dumb *Animal House* peers, at least they had a better sense of themselves than I did. While they lit their farts on fire, I was walking around with an existential dilemma: *How do I exist among these people I don't like?*

I was unreliable to myself. The only thing that was still reliable was alcohol, my only go-to coping mechanism.

* * * * *

My discomfort was seeping into all aspects of my life now. Everyone struggles in that first year away from home—whether they realize it at the time or not—but my struggle seems grotesque in comparison to that of my peers.

It was almost as if I regressed, my high-school bravado slowly eroding despite the fact that I still felt superior to these partying fools.

This was no McDonald's and I was not seven years old. But I felt the same pain as I crossed the floor of the cafeteria. Nobody wanted to sit with me. I could sense it. I couldn't see it, but I imagined their bodies turning away from me as if we were opposite magnets.

I was a pariah again.

The tray with food weighed 100 pounds.

Whatever. I didn't want to sit with those idiots either.

As with my little motorboat, back when I was a boy, I was wrong about what others thought of me standing there with my stupid lunch tray, looking lost. I was accused of being a snob later, of choosing not to sit with people. Meanwhile, I pretended I was cool as I chewed on my sandwich and tried to devise a plan of how to swagger out of the cafeteria in a way that would show everyone I didn't need them or their approval.

* * * * *

During the day, I struggled in classes; my marks no longer so easily scoring in the A or even the B range. But what could a priest or a nun teach me? Please.

I was lying to myself that way, pretending it was the lack of compatibility between me and the curriculum and who taught it that was the reason for my sliding grades.

The real reason was in a bottle. If I did go out, I could revert to my old, high-school ways: a party guru, a clown, a big fun guy who attracts people. But mostly I kept to myself; mostly I just isolated.

* * * * *

In the winter, things started to look up a bit; I almost started to feel at home. Not entirely. But I was adapting in my typical way—I could perhaps make a go of it. I was talking to some people. It was hard for me not to—I was an imposing presence: tall and with a shock of red hair and handsome features. It was impossible to hide in that body. People gravitated toward me naturally.

A ski trip was coming up where I could redeem myself, make everyone forget those allegedly snobbish, better-than-thou cafeteria lunches everyone noticed I was having.

I loved skiing just as I loved any physical activity. Adrenaline remained the most important drug after alcohol for me. There was going to be alcohol on the ski trip, too. In other words, the perfect combination.

I was going with my roommate and three girls. I was looking forward to it. I was looking forward to it so much! One of the girls was especially beautiful and I had a crush on her—I pictured myself schussing down the hill effortlessly, her eyes on me and a small smile on her face as she admired my skills. I pictured myself talking to her later, laughing…making her laugh. Maybe even kissing. Maybe asking her out later. Maybe we could become a thing after this trip.

Four hours until the trip—I couldn't wait! There was a frantic butterfly inside me, euphoria about the adventure spreading into my limbs. I *knew* that this type of euphoria was short-lived, but there was one way to sustain it, and I reached the fridge and grabbed the first can of the evening. It was like pouring liquid gold over that butterfly of euphoria, solidifying it, trapping it. *Now we're talking*, I thought and finished the can.

The van was bouncing with jokes and loud talk, my roommate telling everyone to quiet down, but not really meaning it. I had just said something really funny because the girls burst out with laughter. *What did I say?*

I couldn't remember later. But the girl I liked looked at me with that secret smile and I knew that this trip was going to be epic. I had another beer. Then I wanted to close my eyes. It was funny—my eyelids were exceptionally heavy. But I forced myself to keep my eyes open and cracked more jokes that I couldn't remember later.

Everything was starting to get a little hazy, the swirl that the world seemed to be turning into threatened to pull me inside itself.

How would I ski in this condition? It seemed impossible, but the fresh air would sober me up, wouldn't it? It would. It had to.

It was a difficult task to put the skis on. The bindings kept unbinding themselves and I caught "my" girl looking over at me with a concern on her face instead of a secret smile. I shrugged. "It was so cramped in that car," I said something along the lines of that—blaming my lack of balance on that. The girl smiled.

Finally, it was time to ski. Somehow—a long, black pause—I was on top of the hill and my skis were pointing downward and off I went. I was so...tired that for a split second, I closed my eyes.

What are you doing, David?!

Whoosh, there I was again, back in the world, speeding down. *Idiot.* Even in my wasted brain, I had some sense left to not close my eyes again.

I went up one more time. By the time I got down, instead of sobering up, the alcohol settled in me for good, making my limbs iron-heavy and just as flexible. I could barely move.

Somebody asked me something and I tried to answer, tried to find out what it was that he was asking, but the words wouldn't come out of my mouth.

I was completely wasted. I was done.

How was I going to face my friends?

For now they were at the top of the hill and it seemed they hadn't noticed my state for some miraculous reason. I didn't want them to see me in this state. I pulled my skis off, I stumbled toward the van, I broke the window with a ski—BAM, CRASH—I crawled inside, rolled myself into a ball and passed out.

"David? What's going on? David?" My friends' faces around me, multiplying, circling in that mad spinning of drunk eyes trying to adjust.

"I was cold," I said.

I was cold? What? If I hadn't been so drunk I would've laughed at myself in that moment, but Shame was slowly creeping up on me as I was starting to get sober. No one said anything on the way back; it was as if everything was fine, there was no passed-out David, no broken window, no ruined ski trip. No one said I had disappointed them but they didn't have to. Shame was so great that they might as well have said it—I couldn't possibly face them again.

I couldn't face my roommate now. And I had to live with him.

It was a conundrum.

* * * * *

Other than my roommate and a few acquaintances, I had one friend, another secret introvert like me. We spent some time together, watched TV, talked…he was the only guy I shared anything with. His name was

Pat. But one true connection wasn't enough to quell my anxiety, my growing social phobia.

I drank all the time now—drank to get raving drunk. It wasn't extraordinary because everyone drank, except that I was doing it on Wednesday as well as on Sunday. If I drank around people, there was always someone to be found on any day of the week. Never the same people all throughout the week, and if they were, I didn't notice that. I was aware of only myself drinking almost every day. It's easy to hide when you're an alcoholic in your 20s.

Not that I was an alcoholic—not yet. Or I would still not admit it. True, my grades said otherwise—sliding all the way from As to Cs, but that wasn't a red flag. That was just a hint that I shouldn't have been in that school! I was drinking over that stress, over not being able to fit in, but could you blame me?

All those Bible-thumpers. It was driving me nuts.

I was in the wrong place.

* * * * *

What happens if you're in the wrong place? You find a new place, of course! Because it's never you, it's always the circumstances. An atheist is never going to feel at home in church—it was crazy that I went there. I was not respected.

I was not one of them. Again.

It was no wonder I felt so uncomfortable, barely able to cross the cafeteria floor without crumpling from anxiety.

On top of all of that, the humiliation of the ski trip continued to haunt me and then it was just too much, all of it, and I dropped out. (In the future, I learned that my roommate from the ski trip barely recalled the incident and had no hard feelings toward me.)

* * * * *

To ensure my paranoid self that my humiliation didn't follow me—they would have to lose my scent eventually, no?—I moved more than 1,000 miles away.

The anxiety kept me in its vice-like grip, but as I got closer to St. Petersburg, Florida, I could feel myself relax. Eventually the sun-filled air and the overall cheerfulness of my surroundings—palm trees, beaches, a world-class pier overlooking the city and the ocean— lifted my spirits like a balloon, and I felt almost happy as I entered the new chapter in my life.

My parents' beach house wasn't far away, and my father was finally convinced that this was the right change for me. I sat in on lectures at University of South Florida, unable to get in because of my poor grades. I also took some classes to get in next year. I didn't despair about it because it was a new, happy start and I had all the time in the world.

I had no clothes, no furniture. My drive from Wisconsin was impulsive; it was typical of me and the way I made most of my decisions. I had had enough. Good-bye forever! I didn't look back. What was the point? Being such a skilled adaptee, I never had a hard time molding to the world that kept spitting me out.

Plus, I was sure it was going to be different in Florida. Maybe this was the place for me.

My generous father arranged for my things to be delivered to my new apartment; I was finally on my own, in the place I had picked. I romanticized where I was, who I was going to be. Maybe…Maybe I was going to be an academic star, a genuinely popular guy. Everything would work out in the end and I would no longer feel like a misfit.

Except that living alone was another bottom. I didn't have anybody witnessing my demise. This meant I could drink non-stop and so non-stop I drank. My Cs slid down all the way to Ds. I didn't get admitted to the university. I took more classes and applied again. It was my last attempt, some kind of a reptilian part of my brain that insisted I keep going despite trying to slowly, subconsciously, kill myself. Living on my own was a disaster. I knew then. It was going to finish me off if I didn't do something about it.

* * * * *

Her name was Jackie and she was a slender thing, 110 pounds, five foot nine, blonde, wounded and running away from her pain. She was transparent, real. She became my roommate.

We never became lovers—we joked about it, but we both knew that sleeping together would ruin what we had, which was a real friendship. She was in no state to fall in love anyway, having lost a beloved boyfriend to a motorcycle accident, and I was in no state to fall in love anyway, having already fallen in love with Alcohol, who was a jealous and possessive mistress.

Still, Jackie managed to steal me away from my mistress or at least the connection we developed helped me stay away here and there. I started getting better grades.

I became a full-time student.

I drank less. I limited my drinking to weekends.

Jackie would drink with me, too. She could outdrink me. Maybe she was an alcoholic, too. Maybe her pain was much bigger than mine.

I don't know what happened to Jackie. We lost touch eventually. But our friendship set a blueprint for what I was looking for in people: vulnerability, honesty, integrity. I was so deeply scarred and so afraid of showing it, I knew that I could only learn how to be from people who weren't afraid, like Jackie. She was delicate and strong at the same time—she too was mortally wounded, but she knew where the wound was and why it was and for that I loved her, for letting me into her pain.

* * * * *

There is freedom in letting the world see you for who you really are. The problem was, I still had no idea who I was—I wanted to be seen by the world, but I didn't want to be seen by the world because what was there to show? A son of a red-headed coed, a son of a dark-haired doting mother? A social butterfly, a pariah? A chameleon, a fraud, a lost child? I still didn't know.

The Wolf of the Chicago Board Options Exchange

Have you ever seen a feeding frenzy? Whether in the zoo or in a nature documentary, you must be familiar with what that looks like. I picture piranhas. A tumult of flashing scales, sharp teeth ripping flesh, and blood spewing everywhere, trying to get at the morsel of food as if their lives depended on it. Their lives do depend on it!

My life didn't depend on partaking in frenzy, yet frenzy became my life. The morsels were money, the treacherous piranha-infested Amazon River was the trading floor. It was actually wilder than the Amazon because the frenzy never seemed to end. It went on, round the clock, with people screaming and running, swearing, throwing vulgar jokes intending to hurt, the way piranhas would bite chunks out of one another. I loved it.

It was the perfect place for the kind of guy who one day strapped his windsurfer to the roof of his 1979 Honda Civic, threw his belongings in the back, and gunned it all the way from Florida to Chicago, a 24-hour drive to go after a job he had no guarantee of getting.

Except it was perhaps that sort of attitude—the eagerness I showed—that got me the job. I was on the exchange floor by the time I did my second interview.

It was Thursday and I was starting on Monday. I was going to be a runner, like a piranha living off bits of flesh, $9,000 dollars a year, but it didn't matter. Being here was exactly what I wanted. It was one of those rare times when I was sure of something. I was convinced I would be good at my job—I loved numbers, I loved frenzy, I loved, loved chaos! Especially the kind of semi-controlled chaos that allowed me to thrive.

Within months I was promoted, my responsibilities multiplying as my three bosses figured out that I could easily take over their tasks while they could go and drink. Because that was the irony: I worked for three alcoholics. The sort of guys who yelled at everyone—me excluded for some reason—and who would be drinking by the time 10 a.m. hit, in a bar across the street. I was happy to do their work; I was happy to be thrown into the Amazon River. My confidence was budding; everything felt good. An electric current ran through me day and night. It was almost as good as alcohol, although nothing would ever replace the big A.

I didn't drink during the week—it was puzzling to my bosses who tried to get me hammered with them, but they didn't insist too hard. With four of us drunk there would be no one to do their job.

I was white-knuckling it during the week, and unwinding completely on the weekend. Parallel Universes, Parallel Universes.

After a year of working like a starving piranha, my bonus was $25,000 on top of the measly salary, which wasn't bad at all. Except that the money wasn't really there—the love of my life, Alcohol, was taking a lot of it away.

Eventually, I allowed myself a little treat here and there: a six-pack on the way home, then a six-pack of 16-oz. tall boys. Then more and more...still not on the job, but progressing steadily in how much I was consuming.

The pressure at work became immense, and I continued to love it. I had no coping mechanisms except for drinking and isolating. I was a crazed, happy piranha trying to eat its own tail.

Love

W e met in sailing school when I was eight years old. She was six. It was a beautiful summer, the way all the summers were by the lake. And meeting her didn't seem to add to the specialness of that time, but she was part of it, and it wasn't until years later when I would realize that *she* was my true magic. Unlike fleeting summers and some of the fleeting friendships of those summers, Vicki remained in my life for years and, in fact, she is in my life today.

For a man who has always been haunted by lack of connection, I've been unusually lucky to meet my soul mate that early on and make my most meaningful and deepest connection before I fully knew who I was.

I didn't deserve it. And yet, here it was. Here *she* was.

I don't believe in things like fate-driven coincidences, but it's interesting that as much as I felt I lacked the necessary ingredient (whatever that was) to fit in with the rest of humanity, there were events in my life that left me no choice but to make connections. Meeting my future wife was, naturally, one of those events.

I recall the first time I really noticed her. We were swimming in Lake Beulah as all the lake kids do all summer long—we were like fish, in and out all the time, dripping wet, chasing each other, our laughter echoing all across the water. We were careless and even I was able to relax enough to forget that I was not like them, that there was something wrong with me.

In the summer, on the lake, all those dark worries seemed smaller, almost impossible.

One day, a perfect day, we were all out on the swim raft, a wooden deck with barrels attached to the bottom to make it float. The raft was anchored away from the pier. The weather was blissful with stark-white, billowy clouds in the sky, the sound of water splashing as we threw ourselves around playing sponge tag—a water-soaked cloth that you had to tag friends with, same as on land except in the water. Naturally, you could go under the surface while holding your breath to escape from being tagged.

The sun blinded me and I blinked, and it was in this moment that I saw Vicki as if for the first time. Right before my eyes, she went from being my best friend's kid sister to a beach beauty queen with her bronzed shoulders and sun-bleached, shoulder-length hair. Her wet skin sparkled—it was as if she was covered in it, the sunshine. Her smile, too, radiated when she turned around and our eyes met. I felt some kind of burst inside me, or more accurately, a click—a connection has been made. I swore there was a twinkle in her eye aimed right at me. She was probably all of 12 at the time, and I was 14.

I was instantly smitten. I hoped someone would find me, and she had.

Eventually, we dated as teenagers, when I was 16, but it wasn't really dating. There was some kissing at the end of the night and we held hands, but our meetings were usually in a context of group outings.

We laughed on the boats in the middle of the lake and as she threw her hair back, exposing her throat, the hair like a halo, I was in total awe of her beauty.

I couldn't believe the ongoing transformation that was happening right before my very eyes, how she was changing into a young woman.

I wanted her to myself, but I was careful not to overstep any boundaries. I was in love already without even realizing that's what it was. I kept it inside, secret like everything else in my life—even such a pure, beautiful feeling had to be hidden because I worried there would be consequences were I to let it out. I had good reason to be cautious around her—she was Kent's little sister. And I was a guy with no clear direction and Kent, my close friend—as much as I could bestow that title onto someone back then—knew me more intimately than almost anyone. He knew what kind of guy I was—or I knew what kind of guy I was and I worried that Kent too would have the same opinion about me. I mean, other than getting into small trouble with Kent and partying together, there was the issue of my being less-than, and if I could see it, then Kent could too, right? And why would Kent want his little sister to hang out with a guy like me? Funny, he never actually stood in the way. Those were the stories I was telling myself. I told myself many stories about myself. All kinds of lies.

Maybe that's what helped not to take my infatuation too seriously; also because I remained clueless when it came to relationships.

I worried about overwhelming girls with my neediness. I distanced myself from serious relationships. It wasn't that I wasn't available, but I wasn't that invested; couldn't let myself get invested. I've already disappointed enough people and I got disappointed plenty myself.

* * * * *

There were other girls besides Vicki.

There was drama at an end-of-school party where all the girls I was dating showed up at the same time. Vicki included.

Some tears, some shouting; I was called all kinds of names.

A crowd formed and there I was again, high up in a barber chair, being watched and judged—this time by my closest friends. The girls were furious, with eyes like lasers, burning every time I'd try to look in their direction.

I stopped trying to look. I was embarrassed about my cluelessness: it never occurred to me being an unintentional Lothario would cause any grief. Dating three girls at once? Crazy.

Then again, maybe I wasn't embarrassed enough—I didn't quite feel their pain because to me, it wasn't a huge deal. Perhaps being so consumed with my own self and my insecurity about who I was, I had trouble empathizing. But what young guy is really self-aware enough to know that he's causing heartbreak to someone? Even the most mature ones probably have trouble recognizing all those emotions torpedoing their hearts. And I was not at all a mature or stable teenager.

The fight was short and eventually people dispersed; somebody turned the volume up and there was dancing. I was alone with one of the girls, the most determined one, and not Vicki.

We didn't say much. Her anger was like a radioactive cloud around her.

I didn't want to be at the party any more. But then again, why leave right away?

I should have one more drink.

"Come here," I said to the girl, who didn't leave. She rolled her eyes, strolled over slowly. We clinked our bottles: *To the glorious summer!*

* * * * *

Vicki phoned me in Chicago one evening. I had just gotten home after one of those frenzied, grueling days on the floor. I was exhausted, half in the bag because I had stepped into a bar after work, which wasn't my routine, but once in a while, I had to let my hair down; it was almost expected. My ability to camouflage myself allowed me to pretend I wasn't a big drinker like my bosses, but I knew I needed to strike a balance.

On the phone, Vicki's voice sounded warm and familiar; the warmth hit the sweet spot in my belly like a smoky amber sip of a particularly good Scotch.

"My boyfriend is unable to attend," she explained the situation.

It was a small disaster, and I could tell how much it meant to her, as her voice shook slightly. I knew she was a strong girl, cool-headed, and it was hard to hear her upset.

"I'll come," I said.

"That's why I called," she said. She sounded relieved.

It was spring 1983. My future wife was the social director of her sorority and there was an important house dance. She needed someone to be a safe date for her, someone who would treat her like a gentleman. And since I was that gentleman—I felt a tickle of pride that this was her opinion of me—I was the perfect choice.

I was!

"Saturday."

"Okay, Saturday."

On Friday, there was a jalapeño-eating contest in the local bar and the things were massive, like grenades. They tasted like grenades, too, so it was natural that one would have to drink a lot to quell the fire that hit our mouths and throats before burning its way all the way to our stomachs. So we drank a lot; the gentleman was getting shitfaced.

The gentleman got home at three in the morning and five hours later, the gentleman was driving to Central Indiana from Chicago to accompany Vicki to her dance as her safe, gentlemanly date.

The gentleman showed up with reflective sunglasses, a head that felt seven sizes too big, skin that emitted jalapeño-scented, fermented fumes. Who wouldn't want to go on a date with a gentleman like that?

Vicki had no choice. Years later, she likes to tell the story about her miserable, boring spring house dance date. After the dance, we drove to the hotel I rented for us—without any mischievous intentions; I knew she had a boyfriend—and she was silent the whole time. I slept on the floor.

I. Blew. It.

* * * * *

I wrote letters, sent flowers, stuffed animals. My letters, honest and pained, were full of remorse. It was genuine and it was eating me alive. This was yet another instance where I knew I disappointed so spectacularly that there was possibly no undoing it.

Slowly, her responses became less terse.

Slowly, I could tell, my apologies were making a difference.

Slowly, hope grew in my heart, and it got bigger as the summer approached.

A month later, when Vicki came home for the summer, I asked her out. It was now or never, I knew then. We started to date. Seriously this time.

Two months later, I got down on my knees and proposed to her.

She said yes.

Sometimes all you need is just one person to believe in you. To believe in you more than you believe in yourself.

* * * * *

To marry the woman I loved, I had to break up with my bosses. Or I didn't have to break up with them, but I wasn't going to go to San Francisco where they wanted to open another office and where I was supposed to be going.

In the beginning, I brought up the idea of my working in San Francisco, but Vicki looked at me as if I was crazy—was I actually entertaining living that far apart from each other and somehow making it work? It was baffling to her that it didn't occur to me that our relationship needed nurturing, that I could just believe everything would work itself out because…why? I wasn't sure either. She was right. And I've never felt as connected to anyone as I did to Vicki. Once she pointed out the utopian reality I was suggesting, there was no way I was going to jeopardize our love by living apart from her.

I resigned. Quit the Amazon. I didn't thank my bosses. I didn't explain. Despite the miracle of Vicki believing in me, I was still terrible at human relationships—I had no idea how to enter them or leave them properly. I cut and ran.

It wasn't the most ethical thing to do, but I knew no other way of dealing with it. The idea of disappointing them, of hearing that I failed them was too much to bear—I had no way of knowing they would say that, but it didn't matter.

My first time in the river swimming with the piranhas came to an end. I loved the bloody river and had so much fun there, but it was no longer home. I had a new home now. I was now a man who was loved for who he was, and I was in love, and I was moving to Florida with my beautiful girl, and neither of us had a job or clear idea how we were going to do this, but we had everything we needed: each other and every bit of belief that this was going to work out. And it did.

Life and Death

I met my first blood relative when I was 25 years old. She was a tiny thing with a cloud of red hair and rosebud mouth that opened in a toothless scream as she introduced herself to the world. She was the most beautiful thing I've ever seen. When I held her for the first time, I felt what I'd never felt before: I was no longer floating, no longer half-a-ghost, half-a-man. I was solid. I was getting grounded. I didn't think that in a selfish way—as in *Oh, my daughter is here because her purpose is to help me be in the world*—but it was as if we had been born together.

Up until then, I had no *palpable* evidence of where I had come from. I knew I was adopted, and I knew that my birth mother was too young to have me and that… not a lot more. At that time, there were no pictures. There were the merciful, little half-lies my family told me about the red-headed coed and her football player boyfriend. And, naturally, I knew how I was raised—I had history and memories of my childhood and my adolescent years and those were true enough…but wasn't so much of it built on fiction, too?

Since finding out being adopted was nothing to be proud of, I'd lived my life suspecting deception everywhere.

But now, this beautiful child with red hair and fair complexion was the first truth I witnessed. She was no imaginary university coed, no question mark I shared genes with. She was as solid as the earth I finally felt underneath my feet, no longer floating like that half-a-ghost, half-a-man. She was an affirmation of my belonging to the world after all. It was as if I was finally welcomed to reality: You can stay, David. You just *might* be one of us, the world said.

Yes, the doubt was still there.

But.

There was no denying the existence of my beautiful daughter and our instant bond. There was no doubt there. And that was stronger than anything at that time.

* * * * *

Now that I understood the world better since Adrienne was born, I became a real human being. I was smart and I didn't get too close to people, which allowed me to get by in the world without being exposed for years—exposed that I was a fraud, of course. But now with this baby here, I had a job to do, and that job was to make sure that she was safe; that our whole family was safe. Just as my adopted mother managed to create such a wonderful family life out of ashes of her own tragic upbringing, I would create safety for my daughter where I felt none.

I found a job immediately in Florida as an assistant trader working with institutional clients. It was a natural extension of my job in Chicago. Unlike Chicago, though, this was a suit-and-tie gig and I had to contort myself to look good to the client. Eventually, we moved back to the Midwest to be around my wife's family—it was the right thing to do. Having children affects your lifestyle profoundly and we needed to be closer to our relatives and old friends.

* * * * *

Every time a baby is born, a universe is created. With my daughter, we finally made sense. Not that my wife and I weren't a solid unit, but Adrienne's presence was something that was uniquely ours, our future and a little universe in her own right.

Despite the joy of my daughter's birth, I kept thinking how I had to be careful not to overburden my family with my eagerness to protect them. I had a tendency to do that; in my panic to try to fit in, I pushed people away—I could proverbially suck the air out of the room with my presence.

But so far there was no danger of that; the birth of our daughter brought me and my wife even closer. And my wife, always a strong-minded person, had no problem telling me she needed to be left alone, and I was self-aware enough to not take offense at that.

Overall, she seemed to be better equipped to handle all the changes, mentally at least.

I provided and I partook in domestic duties, but it was Vicki who seemed to know instinctively what she was doing as if she had been given that instruction manual I was so desperately missing.

I was in awe of her ability to switch into this new life with such ease. I wanted to learn how to do that too, and I loved my new life so much that I was careful not to do anything to jeopardize it.

At that time I *still* didn't identify drinking as a problem, so it wasn't something I needed to change, but I did finally think about my values, what I wanted to stand for, what I wanted to pass onto my daughter (and later, my son). It was as if I was entering a new developmental stage—one that most grownups had already aced by the time they were my age.

With this new injection of belief and reflection came confidence. I was confident I was able to provide for my family, I knew I would be able to protect them, and all of that was making me happy. There were many new responsibilities, but also lightness, which I had never experienced.

* * * * *

Our son, Andrew, was born two and a half years later. He was a mini-me: freckles, light hair, same build. Again, I'm not saying that having him was about me—that's what "mini-me" implies, perhaps—but having him was the second time in my life where it was confirmed with no doubt that I was truly alive. That there was a point to my being in the world. And this little person would carry our name forward—it seemed old-fashioned to think that way, but I couldn't help it. I had to grab any confirmation of my existence I could.

Becoming real means that you have to say the words and feel the feelings. Saying you're real doesn't make it so. You need to feel it with your heart.

I was like the Velveteen Rabbit about whom I was reading to my children. A stuffed rabbit sewn from velveteen is given as a present to a little boy, but the rabbit gets snubbed in the beginning in favor of more exciting, mechanical toys. The rabbit finds out that in order to become *Real*, he has to become loved, but knows that he's no competition for all the wonderful toys around him. After one of the cool toys is lost, the rabbit is given to the boy to sleep with at night and it becomes the boy's favorite. When the boy becomes sick, the rabbit is doomed to be burnt with all the toys the boy came to contact with to prevent the spread of the disease. The rabbit cries over missing the boy and a real tear drops onto the ground; a flower spouts. A magical fairy emerges from the flower and she takes the rabbit to the forest where he meets other rabbits and is changed into a real one by the fairy who kisses him. He returns the following spring to look at the boy, to whom the rabbit seems familiar.

I read the story a hundred times as a young father, but it never occurred to me how obvious the message in it was. Like the Velveteen Rabbit, I was loved by my adoptive family and, later, I was loved by the family I created—and I was healing from my disconnect, unbeknownst to myself. Sure, there were many moments when I didn't feel quite real. I drank over those moments, but during the first few years of my children's lives, my drinking didn't take away the safety I've tried so hard to give them. I was a velveteen rabbit not entirely comfortable in his own skin, but I didn't turn into an unsafe alcoholic for a long time. I didn't take the safety away from my kids…yet.

What Is Real?

Have you ever had a dream where you're one thing and then another, and then you are both things, but you're also the thing that kills both those things, but you are also alive and you also know you're dreaming?

This was akin to my state of mind most of my life—even in those sweet days of starting a family. I wasn't psychotic, and I knew what was real and what wasn't—my son's belly laughter was real, my daughter's coy smile was real—but with time, the dream like confusion enveloped me again.

The thing about the human psyche is that we can hold it all together for a time—months, even years sometimes—but whatever demon we try to ignore will always find us and drag us down. Mine was, of course, my lack of solid identity or the identity shifting, threatening my very existence.

My wife has a deep lineage, way past the American Revolution, signatures in a family Bible from 200 years ago. We couldn't be more opposite when it came to our pasts, which didn't create a chasm between us, but it was impossible to ignore now that there were children.

For practical reasons, too. I had no knowledge of any specific genetic legacy other than how my children looked. I myself haven't suffered from any illnesses, but there are secrets out there that skip generations and bestow themselves on people unannounced. It would be irresponsible not to try to find my family's history. My wife urged me to and I felt guilty about not doing anything about it.

So the same theme went on in my life—guilt turning into Shame—and once Shame took over, it was like swallowing a grenade and having it explode inside. Suddenly, there was so much damage that I didn't know where to start repairing it.

The more time passed, the bigger Shame grew— maybe there was something so wrong with me that I had to be relinquished, maybe I was some kind of a monster baby, maybe—I couldn't think about it. My children were perfection. I couldn't allow myself to investigate my past and bring from it a potentially devastating element that would sentence them—and me too—to some kind of horror I couldn't imagine. That's the thing about fear—it can be irrational, bigger than the threat, especially if it's imagined the way I kept imagining it. The way that nightmare dream is where you're one thing and then another and then both things and then…

* * * * *

Years later, after finding out about where I came from, I learned an important lesson. The lesson was that, although it mattered where I came from, it didn't mean I would get the kind of closure that would wrap my life up with a bow. When I finally got some information about my roots, I still couldn't deal with who I was or wasn't. It's funny—people chase after closure so intensely they forget to actually live their lives. We are not movies with credits rolling after every scene.

To me, eventually learning where I came from only gave me perspective as to what had shaped me. It didn't cure me. And, at the time of my children's arrivals, information simply seemed like a threat—a door I was afraid to kick open because I've already had enough monsters to deal with, and what if the one behind the door was the scariest and biggest one of all?

Selling My Soul

I was back in the river full of piranhas, standing in the pit at 6:00 a.m., taking up space that wasn't mine.

In 1986, I moved with my family to Chicago to work with my friend and brother-in-law, Kent. I was hired to help him keep his trading position in order and to facilitate his actual trading in the pit.

Pit trading is a young person's game, as it is mentally and physically demanding. But I was young and I was ready to go. I was full of energy; it seemed to have doubled now that I had a family to protect and provide for. There was finally a reason for me to be making all this money, and if I was going to make money, I wasn't going to do it half-assed. So I stood in the space that belonged to two other traders, "Neil" and "Bob." A joke popped into my head.

When the traders, Neil and Bob, showed up and demanded for me to move, I threw an insult that made the entire trading floor laugh: "Kneel and bob, is that what you guys do here?"

I was abusive. But that was the deal. I had to be the big, abusive guy making jokes. Piranhas biting each other. Tearing each other apart.

Within a year, I was trading on my own with Kent sponsoring my membership to the Chicago Board Options Exchange (CBOE), providing the money that enabled me to trade my own position and hiring a clerk to replace me.

As the operation grew, we continued to hire clerks, traders, computer programmers, quantitative analysts. We were wildly profitable. We were wild. I could feel the blood rushing through my veins, going faster, harder. I was becoming a big trader in the Chicago pits again. I was being watched. I had people wanting to take me down. I was sitting in the Big-boy barber chair and every hair on the back of my neck stood up straight and I couldn't show it.

There was no danger of anyone getting too close anyway. In my typical vein of living a parallel life, on the trading floor, I was a professional, serious, non-drinking bully who postured all the time. Distance was my game. There was an invisible, radioactive field around me. I shouted numbers, I sweated, rolled sleeves, and outshouted everybody, and I couldn't wait to get to my apartment or on the plane and claim my reward—the hiss and the bliss of that first drink.

* * * * *

I got stopped once in 1989, when I came to with my body all beat up, my tongue swollen and screaming with pain inside my mouth. I had no idea what had happened. It was the middle of the night.

Vicki, panicked beside me in our bed, shouted my name over and over.

The doctors had an answer for me right away. It was the Optifast diet. That's what had caused the seizure.

It made sense. One of the things that bothered me about my life back then was my weight. Despite all the adrenaline, all the jumping on the trading floor, I wasn't slimming down—my lifestyle meant late meals and stress-eating and snacking, and the beers didn't help either. I didn't pay attention to what I was consuming—there was simply no time. So when Oprah endorsed the diet, it was suddenly everywhere, inescapable. The 18-week strict program focused on nutrition, behavior, and medical assessments, included meal replacement drinks and bars and counseling. I sat in group sessions and silently judged my fellow dieters, who kept cheating and stuffing their faces with food—unlike me, who didn't even have a bite of a raisin. (Years later, I realized that I was cheating all along—I drank like a fish, consuming empty calories and not giving it another thought.)

I ended up losing 87 pounds. I was a success. Of course I was a success. As with everything else, I immersed myself in the program. Sadly, I found myself in my bed coming out of a seizure shortly after that success, my tongue bitten to shreds.

My body was starving. It couldn't take the strict (non)-eating regime.

I was really disappointed that it was the diet that caused this. A doctor suggested I should sue, but I let that go—I just wanted the whole thing to disappear: the diet, the seizure, and Shame I've felt over what I considered a baffling failure.

I threw myself back into recklessness, back into the darkest depths of the river with my fellow piranhas. Soon enough I forgot all about the diet that had betrayed me so greatly. Soon enough I was spinning like a madman, cured from my seizure, high on adrenaline again, and booze, going, going, going, going—running away from myself and chasing, never stopping to think about what it was that I was running away from and chasing.

* * * * *

On the weekends, I was an entirely different animal. Or not an animal. More like half-a-human: exhausted from his workweek with bleary eyes and body that could never quite unwind. I would have to be back in Chicago on Monday.

I drove 96.5 miles to and from work—three hours in traffic between Chicago and our Lake Beulah home. There was no room for mistakes.

I reserved my drinking for the weekends, which, sadly, were the only days I could spend time with my family. So my drinking took me out of the family unit. I was there in body, but it was as if I wasn't there at all. I don't know if my children could tell what was going on with me. I wondered if my wife could tell, but she was always cool and composed, and it was as if she watched me from a distance. I remember only occasional remarks about my overindulgence, but they came from her caring about me, not because she wanted to shame me.

I don't believe my wife was an enabler. She was simply busy maintaining our home and taking care of our children, and she was perhaps too busy to babysit me as well. And I didn't feel as if I needed babysitting. As far as I was concerned, I was just taking the edge off, but the edge was getting bigger and bigger.

A Driving Problem

I wasn't sure what happened. I had always been a good driver, but one night in February, I plowed into a guardrail in my Mercedes Benz 500S. I couldn't back off the guardrail and the car was stuck. Some helpful soul called the police who came to help. I mean, arrest me.

I explained to the cop how I had driven 30 miles to Milwaukee that Friday evening to watch the NBA Milwaukee Bucks. I didn't mention that I met up with some Wisconsin friends, where we drank heavily before and during the game, then went out to the bars afterward. There is no way I should have been driving, but I was. Which is why I missed a turn two miles from my home and was now one with the guardrail.

I managed to keep my name out of the papers. I had a reputation to live up to as big-shot David, and I wasn't about to ruin it by making a driving mistake. I needed to prove to those around me that I meant business when it came to getting better. To show my commitment, I took DUI classes and I aced them.

I wrote the greatest essay on drinking and driving in the history of essays on drinking and driving. I graduated and everything was fine until six months later when I had another driving situation.

This time, I was in a car with three people who didn't know about my driving problem. I remember their worried faces—"Shit, David"—and I remember doing what I do best—pretending everything was fine. "It's okay, guys," I said something along the lines of. It wasn't okay. They had no idea about my first DUI. But the cop did.

He pulled me aside. He must've had a really good day, or maybe I had a really good day—it's hard to decide now. The cop looked at me and I waited for the bomb to explode. Instead, he sighed, "I want you to call someone to get you."

I wanted to kiss him, that's how grateful I felt. He was the best cop I've ever met. A real chap.

Another DUI wouldn't fly under the radar; there would be no more attorneys to stop the presses.

From then on, I reduced my driving and started taking taxis and limousines if I needed to get around. I drank and I kept drowning, but somehow I was lucky enough to never fully drown. I was a piranha, after all.

The Rest of My Life

I think of a dialogue from the movie *Animal House* between Boon and Katy.

Katy: *Is this really what you're gonna do for the rest of your life?*

Boon: *What do you mean?*

Katy: *I mean hanging around with a bunch of animals getting drunk every weekend.*

Boon: *No! After I graduate, I'm gonna get drunk every night.*

* * * * *

I was now a full-on graduate of life. A real grownup. I'd finally reached the point in my life where making money went from necessity to pleasure to necessary obsession—another thing that fed my need for adrenaline.

Our business was expanding. Up until then, we had focused exclusively on the Chicago markets, but there was a golden opportunity to expand to foreign markets. We hired an investment bank to represent us in finding a strategic partner who had financial infrastructure in these foreign markets, yet who wanted our money-making expertise in these options and futures (often referred to as "derivatives") markets.

After that, we inked a deal with a London-based international investment bank to lead their worldwide derivatives trading operation (they had no derivatives operation up to that point). We were compensated with a combination of cash, incentive options, and deferred payments, including our agreement to five-year employment contracts with the investment bank.

My partner and brother-in-law moved to London to assume his role as head of worldwide derivatives operations, and I found myself in New York leading North American operations and sitting on the bank's New York Board of Directors.

I was 33. I was a punk. I was a king. Two different things again. All I knew was how to make money and how to be still under the microscope of the world. It was necessary—the sitting still, the quiet storm inside me—to annihilate any doubt in anyone's mind whether I was the right guy to do the job I was doing. It's not that I wasn't confident in my abilities—just the opposite. I thrived in that confidence—but I was never sure of when people would see through me, see the relinquished boy inside me who was scared and ashamed. He was like a little ghost, perched on that barber chair, always there.

I often got the dry heaves from nerves before having to speak to rooms of people. Saying "no" to people I was trying to adapt to was not an option.

Later, I reflected how I'd constantly put myself in these positions—what was it? Courage or insanity? I still don't know.

But for now, I was in New York, performing my gig of being Big Bad David, sitting on that Board with Sirs and Lords and Masters and all kinds of royalty I knew and cared nothing about.

I was flying to and from New York, where I quickly rented an apartment in Manhattan.

I would start drinking in the Admiral's Clubs, then on the plane, getting home already buzzed. If I had the energy, I would drink with some friends back home and fly back hung over to later drink alone in my apartment after a whole day of white-knuckling—not drinking—in the office and thinking of that first drop sliding down my throat.

There was so much going on. So many different lives. Not two, but three or four even, 60-hour work weeks, blasted-away weekends.

I had two houses already. That apartment in Manhattan.

I was on the plane. I was off the plane.

I was in my wife's arms. I was leaving to drink with friends on the lake.

I was drunk, half-drunk, completely sober, but full of adrenaline like a drug.

I was hung over, miserable.

Happy.

I was aggressive and polite. I had no idea how to behave, so I behaved as if the world was watching. Or I hid from the world so it would stop watching me.

My life was divided by suitcases, closets, secret bottles, papers. The papers that gave me paper cuts so deep occasionally I'd have to stifle a sob when I received yet another fax of my children's art project as I'd put in long hours in the office.

I had no idea how to stop working and change my life so that I would finally start participating in it properly.

My exhaustion was like a big, black cloud swallowing me. David was disappearing. As time went on, I was becoming more and more alone, unable to see people socially during the workweek because I constantly worried about my reputation—the biggest drunk was sober to that world.

Always in line with the theme in my life, I've lived as I thought others expected me to live. It wasn't a bad thing, of course, to keep up those professional appearances—my job was dependent on how I presented myself physically and how I conducted myself—but it was killing me.

There were times when I almost forgot who I was, *why* I was, whose custom-made shirts those were in the strange closet.

I missed everything—my family most of all—but also the adrenaline and the money that kept coming, making me into a zombie. The zombie would be back home for the weekends.

* * * * *

Two years into our partnership, the London investment bank sold itself to a bigger international bank and we were asked if we'd like to buy ourselves back to get our trading operation off of its books. We did, accelerating our compensation and ending our five-year employment contracts after only two years. With a big chunk of money in my pocket, I decided I had worked hard enough for long enough, and was now ready to give it a break. I immediately came home.

* * * * *

"What do you want to do?"

"One house," Vicki said.

"One house?"

"One house."

Vicki meant the Pine Lake house in Chenequa, where she was about to reside with the children and where they went to school. We sold our Chicago house. The Pine Lake home was a less seasonal lake house, more inland anyway, and picking one place meant we would finally be a complete family again. We decided to sell our house on Lake Beulah—her family still had theirs there, so the lake would remain in our lives— and we decided I would give up my apartment in Manhattan (gladly).

- 80 pairs of underwear
- 4 electric toothbrushes

- 25 business suits
- 50 custom-made shirts

Shoes, socks, coats. Enough to fill three different closets, but now, finally, all of that, all of my fragments combined and in one place. There was going to be one David only, too—the family David who had a golden ticket to life, in an almost literal sense.

Golden Ticket

I partied for 10 years…until the next day. The next day didn't come until my mid-40s, but when it did—well, we won't get into that yet.

For now, I was David the Fun Guy again, just like I had been in high school, except this time I had what should have been a lifetime supply of dollars in my pocket, a family, and a demon the size of the lake where I partook in most of my drinking.

Being 35 and on top of your game and never having to work? I was finally the quintessential Boon from *Animal House*—I could do whatever I wanted and there was no one who could stand in my way.

I was also the ultimate dad now—always there for my kids, eating breakfast with them, going to their after-school events, their games, their sailing school and regattas. I was not like all the other dads, barely able to loosen their ties, always struggling to find time. I was gregarious, generous, and full of life.

Other than that, I had no accountability. At least in Chicago or New York I couldn't drink in front of people because I had to remain professional and alert, but here, on the lake? I could do whatever the hell I wanted. And I aligned myself with people who partied like me.

"You're drinking too much," my wife would say sometimes.

"I've got it under control," I would say back. I had it under control.

I had it under control.

Vicki would say nothing back. What would be the point? Sometimes I would even convince her everything was fine with my confident declarations. That's what I believed.

It turned out later she knew I was an alcoholic long before I did. I wasn't fooling anybody except for myself. But there was no way anything Vicki would say would force me to look at myself. It wasn't her. She was familiar with my general avoidance. She witnessed how I coped with life or how I didn't cope with it. She could see that I wasn't ready to deal with my darkness. But it wasn't her not being able to say anything—it just wouldn't register. We both knew it.

I loved her. Very much. I loved my kids. Very much. They were everything to me—my family. And now I was finally free to be with them, full time, after all those weeks of absence, the 60-hour-work weeks and faxing our love back and forth like it was business. We no longer had to live like that. We could now enjoy each other fully, presently. Our love for one another was in the room with us, not miles away. It was special.

But after dinner, if there were no friends to drink with, I would slither off to my office for a rendezvous with my True Love, Alcohol, the most important of them all.

I never realized that there was a competition, but of course, there was. My family was abandoned upstairs and me alone with my True Love, a possessive, demanding mistress who wouldn't take "no" for an answer. Not that I would ever say "no" to her.

* * * * *

Now that I was no longer in the do-do-do-go-go-go mode, I had to find ways to occupy my mind, which continued going at full tilt. Just because I didn't have to go to a job, it didn't mean that my brain had retired as well.

Picture me sitting at the end of a pier watching the lake, the sunset. The romance of nature all around me. The calm that is almost tangible. It was June. The temperature was perfect: warm but not too hot. My lungs filled with air so clear, I could feel myself getting healthier as I breathed it all in. No more airports and board meetings and jumping in the pit like a hungry piranha. Peace.

This is it, I said to myself. *Be quiet, this is what you wanted. This, right here.*

But my brain wouldn't stop talking back to me, *What should I do...what should I do...what should I do?*

Stop it. I don't have to do anything. I don't have to be anywhere the next day. This is what life is about, right? Enjoying it. Enjoy life! How many people get to do it? Not many. And I got to where I was myself—I have achieved more by 35 than most people in their entire lifetimes. I'm so happy. So relaxed. This is so relaxing.

What should I do?

I should relax. I'm relaxing. I'm so relaxed.

I'm not on the airplane, now what? Now what? Am I going to just sit here for 40 more years? What should I do? How did this happen? I don't know who I am. What to do? Why don't I know who I am? I was a trader—who am I now? Who am I? What should I do? What to do? What to do, what to do, what to do? What should I do? What should I do? What should I do?

This is great, look at this beautiful sunset, oh, the soft warm breeze is so nice against my skin.

What should I do? What to do what to do whattodo-whattodowhatodo…I gotta keep moving, you gotta move right now, move it before something hits you.

I got up and went back to the house to get a drink. Screw relaxing.

* * * * *

And so it became clear to me that I no longer had the identity I aligned myself with: that of a big-shot. All gone. Lots of money in my pocket but now what? The great trader, the one everyone was watching—a great promise and success on the Chicago trading floors? I was no longer him, but then who was I?

I was again lost in my own life.

I should probably talk to someone about this, I thought more than once, *but who would I talk to and what would I say?*

I could talk to Vicki, because she possibly understood more about me than I understood about me, but I had no idea what it was that I would tell her. I couldn't figure out how I felt. Did I feel good? I felt good. Great, even. Then why the despair and the sitting and wistfully watching the lake, trying to enjoy the calm of it while my mind spun madly inside my skull? I had no idea. The only idea I had was that there was a way to calm that storm, and so I kept drinking.

* * * * *

I was confused and in pain, but I wasn't unhappy—I only had to find a way to occupy myself and everything would work out. It was normal to go into a bit of shock after such a significant life change, retiring. All I needed right now was comfort. And ease. Or all together: ease and comfort so that I could ease myself into this new phase. I would immerse myself in ease and comfort!

Ease and Comfort

The best way to achieve the ultimate ease and comfort is to plan a business trip less than a month into your retirement. Nothing relaxes a person more than a grueling schedule of meetings and travel soaked in ridiculous amounts of booze. Well, the booze wasn't planned, exactly, but it would always find its way into my life and the insidious thought of it was in the back of my mind before I even announced to my family that I was leaving. The thought was: *I get to get away with drinking because nobody will be there to watch me.*

"Kids will be going to a new school...maybe we should help them to prepare...you've only just retired... maybe you should take a break...", Vicki was saying but it wasn't really registering. It was echoing somewhere in my head, like a distant buzz, trying to pierce through but not succeeding, coming up against the resistance of the thoughts about drinking with impunity.

My friend Peter convinced me to go to on a business trip with him. He was the biggest importer of granite in the United States. He needed to visit mining companies in Southern India, and I was good with numbers and had lots of useful business skills. Maybe we could make this a go—or I could get involved part-time.

The ideas weren't quite formed; they were just something I was lying to myself about to give myself permission and reason to go on this trip.

It should be impossible to lie to yourself—after all, you already know the truth!—yet many of us are able to do it and I was a master at it. Denial.

I've been lying to myself all my life or, more accurately, I've felt my life was a lie because of my mysterious origins. It was easier for me to lie to myself than it would be for a man who knew exactly who he was. Yes, I had morals and values and I was deathly aware of all this unresolved chaos within me, but I was also a paradox in that way—I wasn't sure if those were my values and morals because I'd been adapting to my environment for so long. So what exactly were my values?

What was the reality?

Was reality relative? Specifically: was my going to India a true urge to get involved in a real business venture, or was it an excuse to not be accountable (and drink)? Or both?

I packed my suitcase.

* * * * *

Peter and I decided to make a little stop in Rome before going to Bombay. There are no direct flights to India from the U.S., and I've always wanted to check out the

Vatican. I was not religious, but I have an immense respect for history and the Vatican was on my bucket list.

I forget where we started. A restaurant, probably, and we probably had something delicious, a pasta dish or pizza or ravioli or chewed-up bottom of a shoe, who could really tell. I couldn't. There were drinks—wine and more wine and later, drinks for everybody and tips for everybody, and then we were outside and getting in a taxi and going to a club. Somebody was coming with us—a waiter from the restaurant or maybe a tourist we ran into while catching the taxi. Somebody else was ushering us through a dark alley, and then we were in a club with lights and booming music and there were more drinks—drinks for all the nice people at the bar and more tips for all the nice bartenders and the music was getting louder. I didn't know I could move to the rhythm so well, but it turned out in Italy, I was an exceptionally good dancer, and so I danced with my glass. Next to me someone was topping it with Champagne.

Who bought the Champagne?

I bought the Champagne! There was laughter—men and beautiful women, everyone young and tanned and bursting with life. Bodies covered in sweat and more Champagne! More!

Bubbles everywhere, the lights blinding me, the music still pounding. My buddy screaming in my ear that we were going somewhere else, somewhere better. Yes! We had to get out of here—the place was getting too crowded and the night was young. Where were we now? Oh, Scotch. What an expensive Scotch—was it expensive? I tried to convert lira into dollars, but it was pointless; I couldn't keep the numbers in my head long enough to make them stick. So back in the taxi we went, or maybe we just walked—we walked to one place for sure, not sure where we were before we walked there; maybe the place where we had the expensive Scotch. This place...this one was just a smear of red neon lights and glasses clinking and cigarette smoke. This place was too smoky, but then there was another place, a patio, and we were sitting at a table with some people and I thought I could speak Italian, or they were all speaking excellent English. We were having a great conversation and a great time and someone was paying for all of this; I was. You only live once.

The lights outside were yellow and pleasantly buzzing, like little suns, in the warm night speeding through my veins as we hopped to another place, and then everything went from a blur to just dark, and the next thing I knew, I was in my hotel room having a nightcap.

I woke up drunk, a few thousand dollars poorer—not that it mattered.

I showered and dressed, feeling *it* slowly creep in, starting somewhere in the top of my head and my guts, like slow death. I could tell that within hours, *it* would attack fully and there will be no going back—there never was going back. None of the cures worked. But I had no choice. I couldn't spend the day lying in the hotel room with the blinds closed. We had a flight to catch. We were going to Saudi Arabia, one more stopover.

I moved slowly as if through molasses as I made my way downstairs and then into a taxi. I had no idea what the Vatican looked like. The taxi lurched forward. I closed my eyes.

Peter seemed to be okay. He complained of a headache, but when I finally managed to lift an eyelid, he was looking out the window, fresh and happy as a clam. I didn't know how much he drank. Had he even been drinking after the first part of the night, the part where we were maybe in a restaurant? Had he— ?

I couldn't even think. It was better not to think. I closed my eyes again. The headache was now overwhelming—it seemed bigger than my head. I was inside the headache. I was the headache.

I was going to be sick. I was hoping to be sick. In the past, when I had a hangover like this, being sick would sometimes help. But somehow, I wasn't able to get sick even though my guts twisted inside me. I wanted to die. I didn't really want to die, but I wanted it to end. I started making bargains with myself: never again, never like that, no more mixing, never mix…By the time we got to the airport, I was sure I would never drink.

I looked down at my hands and noticed that my wedding ring was missing.

I pictured it clearly then. Right beside the sink in the hotel room. What kind of man forgets his wedding ring? A bad man.

I called from the airport but the ring was gone.

I was a bad man. I prided myself on being organized, mathematical, careful, but there it was—a white band of un-tanned skin around my finger where the ring used to be.

On the flight to Saudi Arabia, I tried to sleep but couldn't—even sleep hurt, although that was what I desperately wanted. Please, please, please…if I could only get a few hours in my hangover would lessen.

"You smell like a liquor store," my friend laughed beside me.

In Saudi Arabia, when we got off the plane, I was convinced for a moment I was hallucinating from my hangover. There were guys with machine guns in the corridor. I was hoping to get some fresh air but I was scared to go past them, so we waited for the plane to India, and then we were back on the plane.

Getting off the plane in India, my hangover was still in full tilt. My walk toward the taxi stand was a death march. I would've prayed if I hadn't been an atheist. I felt I was truly in hell: the heat, the smells, the chaos, the colors, the people, so much of everything, all of it swirling around me as I could barely keep my eyes open. I was going into day two of my hangover. The heat was burning my skin off; I was sugar and ferment and I blended in with all the smells, and I made some more promises to never drink again, and then off we were, driving to Southern India toward the granite and marble mills.

By the time we got to our destination, my hangover had evaporated and I felt as if I had just run a marathon—my body destroyed, but on its way to recovery now.

We were led to our accommodations with flushing Western toilets and expensive sheets and air conditioning and every luxury a person could want; we were treated like royalty. That was exactly the opposite to how people in villages around here were living, with a hole in the ground for a toilet, the heat always relentless, the smells of death and rot and food always there.

But now wasn't the right time to think about all that. I was exhausted and, although my hangover had subsided, I felt delicate and unsure, like it, the hangover, could come back any moment. I lay down gingerly and closed my eyes.

After my nap, I felt even better. Almost reborn. I splashed some cold water on my face. I went downstairs to meet my friend. Then we were on our way to meet his prospective business partners.

Then it was Johnnie Walker Blue label and BOOM, there it was again.

I hesitated for a brief second. Next the burning gold was sliding its way down my throat.

Criterion Number 5

In the *DSM-5* Criteria for Alcohol Use Disorder, there are eleven markers that indicate a maladaptive use of alcohol (alcohol use disorder) if at least two to three of them are met within the same 12-month period. In the beginning of the 10-year-long phase of my retirement, I could probably be summed up and identified by number five on that list: "Recurrent alcohol use resulting in failure to fulfill major role obligations at work, school, or home."

They say hindsight is 20-20 and at the time, I was still in enough denial to manage to lie to myself effectively enough that I'd never called myself on my own bullshit. What bullshit? I was just a social, gregarious guy who had money to spend and time and energy to live life to its fullest potential. I was the guy to go to if you wanted to have a wild weekend; I threw the best parties. If you think about it, I really had *no* choice but to surround myself with alcohol.

I threw myself into the pursuit of partying with as much fervor as I used to have on the trading floor. Probably even more since I had more freedom now to be myself. I still didn't have the kind of freedom that would allow me to drink without scrutiny—my wife and my children were around me all the time—but the boundaries were looser and all I had to do is figure out how to maneuver within those boundaries. In other words, I had to find good, solid excuses for always stocking up such copious amounts of booze. Explanations in case anybody asked. No one did.

Sometimes in my double-think there would be a flash of worry, but it was only a flash, and then it was back to my delusions. If there was no reason for a party, there would have to be a reason found—I had already stocked up for it!

* * * * *

It is difficult to explain to non-addicts how much our lives—the addicts' lives—are ruled by the substances they abuse. The substance—in my case, alcohol—was my love; the sun that the Earth revolved around, if you care for more metaphors. It was essential to always be in its orbit, otherwise it seemed to me I could cease to exist. But it was also important to not acknowledge how much I relied on it—in the same way that we don't acknowledge the sun, I could pretend that alcohol had no great influence on my life. I could tell myself it was there to simply aid my social persona, nothing else. It wasn't a source of life; it wasn't my sun.

* * * * *

I stayed put in Wisconsin after India—at least stayed on the same continent for the most part. But it was too quiet after India, on top of it already being very quiet after my life as a trader, and now both of those silences echoed loudly as I tried to come up with something to occupy myself.

I was socializing, of course. Non-stop. Drinking with others, I was chasing connections, but I was, as usual, worried about what people thought of me. In a way nothing has changed from my high school years when that was my M.O.

And as it was in high school, alcohol facilitated instant bonding; it was the magic elixir that never failed, although the older I got, the harder it was to deny that the elixir had poisonous qualities to it. The hangovers were a physical manifestation of the toxicity of it, but then there was also my wife's downturned mouth and my children's unsure eyes as they looked at me coming through the front door. *What kind of husband, father are we getting tonight?* I tried not to see them looking at me like that. I remembered those looks years later, in sobriety. There was undeniable sadness and anger and my alcoholism was what was causing it.

* * * * *

For now, I made more plans, more trips for the off-season, and there were still lots of parties to throw that would tide me over during the periods of inactivity. My wife and I ran the junior sailing school; we brought people to our property and continued to entertain.

Incidentally, I was horrible at attending family celebrations such as Christmas or birthdays because I couldn't drink prior to those events, and during, I couldn't drink too much. I had to be careful not to get sloppy around my relatives, my in-laws, my own parents. I was, as always, living the double life of David. The way I wanted people to see me, and the way I really was. If I could get away with it, I'd claim illness and stay home with my True Love, my Sun, my Alcohol—just us, left alone without anybody watching and judging.

* * * * *

Despite the fact that I remained in denial about how much I drank, it was clear to me that my normal, everyday life tended to get in the way of my drinking. Not that anyone was standing in the door preventing me from leaving, but I was too self-conscious to drink openly in front of my family all the time. I loved spending time with them, and derived a lot of joy from being a father, and from being able to be there for many of my children's sporting events, but to be honest, I was also always looking forward to when I could check out and do my own thing. Kids can sense these things; they can sense inattention. I've always had such close connection to my own childhood, I should've been more aware of how I was with my own family, but there's no such thing as a self-aware addict in the throes of addiction. There's only delusion.

To get away from them—and from the shame over not wanting to be with them all the time, too—I spent a lot of time in my basement office. I was there under the pretext of looking for a business idea on the Internet. There was no business to be found. None of the ideas I came across would interest me enough. Or perhaps I just wasn't sober enough to notice something that would normally pique my curiosity. It was hard to see through the blur of intoxication.

Sometimes there would be notes that made no sense the next day—despite that at the moment of putting them on paper, I was convinced I was about to come up with the greatest invention since the telephone. *David, you are not afraid to make mistakes! You've got this*, I would drunkenly pep-talk myself.

But all I was, was a man with a tumbler of whiskey in one hand, trying to balance on my ergonomic chair—a drunk surfer of the Web. A TV on, a fresh 12-pack of Heineken, too, in the fridge, and me and my blurry ideas.

I thought I was great.

I was an egomaniac with an inferiority complex.

The next day, the scribbles were impossible to decipher, but if I managed to decipher them, it would be too embarrassing to read what I had written.

I thought a lot and I drank a lot.

I drank a lot and I thought less.

I drank to quiet my mind.

So I drank because I had to.

And I drank because I wanted to.

And because I needed to.

* * * * *

I didn't just sit in the basement and drink—as I mentioned I needed a variety of reasons to justify my drinking. So there were excursions. Football games that started at 7:00 p.m. that my buddies and I would leave for at noon even though it would take less than three hours to get there. On the way, you could visit a few bars, have a few. The limo would wait outside.

By the time we'd get to the games, our own game was fully on. And we'd drink during the game, too, cheer on, drunkenly, obnoxiously. Then we'd drive back, a few more for the road—a few more before bed. Sometimes we would make it a two-night thing, a weekend thing and my mind would be numbed with drink to the point of total ease and comfort and total blotto. No more thinking.

In the winter, it would be snowmobile trips—my truck loaded with my big-boy toys, riding 150 miles a day, rock'n'roll ripping through the trails, going from bar to bar before getting to our destination. I was often the driver—in more ways than one. I would organize the trip, I would plan the stopovers, I had the equipment. I was in charge. I was in control. Of everything. I was always afraid of running out—of booze, of fun— and I had to keep going and going, and my exhausted buddies could barely keep up with me. But they did because the trips were glamorous and exciting and who doesn't want to have fun forever?!

There would be three times as much booze as there would be food for a four-day weekend. There would be cases instead of one bottle. My friends smiling unsurely, a glimpse of *what-the-hell?* in their eyes.

"What?"

"Nothing, nothing, David. That's a lot of booze."

"Is it?"

I wasn't so sure. I thought, *I just do things bigger and better than most people, that's all.* I never wanted to run out. I wanted to have a great time—I had a great time. I can't say it wasn't great. The connection was there, the freedom was there: big, overwhelming, intoxicating, as we sped toward the next adventure.

There were times I wished I could somehow just stay out forever, not have to come home. I loved my home, I loved my family! I knew that at home the reality was closer than it was while driving drunk in a Suburban full of drunk buddies and beaten-up machines. There was laughter, teasing, recounting of our weekend away…it was so much fun. I felt the love all around me. We were in this together.

I was so alone.

There was only me.

Sailing

I threw myself into sailboat racing, too. I sailed like a madman for four years until I herniated two disks in my back, which ended my sailing career.

Before that happened, though, half the year's boredom was taken care of right then and there. Sailing was something I could do every weekend, from April to September. I stayed on the home lake for some of the races, but other times, I traveled with my crew to places like Texas or New York State or Iowa—all over the country really–to attend every regatta. We became known as "road warriors."

I loved sailing. It was in my blood, having grown up on a lake.

Often the boat felt like an extension of my body; I understood the link between the boat and myself and the water, and I could make it all interlock perfectly, drive it toward winning the race. I loved the connection with the water, how I felt myself aligned with the 38-foot sailboat called *Piranha*. I steered her toward victory with a crew of five or six people. It was a powerful and beautiful experience, and miraculously, there were a few rare moments while doing that when I didn't think of the sweaty cold neck of a beer bottle, when I only thought about the speed and the open space ahead of me.

The thing about sailing is that you need to always pay attention, be mindful of the weather, the water, the crew—there's no room for distractions. But distractions happen. When we stopped paying attention some-times, the boat would capsize, overturn, end our race. Sometimes it would only tip over to the side, but then other times it would "turn turtle"—go upside-down fully—from a speeding wing to a floating slow shell.

My life resembled those aspects of sailing. Some-times I would go at full tilt, joyful with waves splashing all around me, my happy heart feeling like it could burst out of my chest, but then one wrong turn and I was tip-ping over, capsizing. Floating miserably like a turtle.

I don't know if my friends drank as much as I did at the regattas. But even an addict in denial occasionally questions his drinking—or challenges it in the way that he always hopes that he's not the one drinking the most. And if he is—and he *always* is—it's not hard to tell your-self otherwise. The best thing to do is to not watch how much others drink and get any sort of hang-ups about being the thirstiest.

* * * * *

Even though I considered myself a sailor, it wasn't until I had some clarity to look back and admit to myself that, often, what was more exciting about the sailing was the cooler of beer I packed for the day.

I'm being a little unfair to myself. I *was* a sailor. Or a part-time sailor, because once I actually calculated the number of days I'd spent on the water racing— it was 14 days in one year. Weather was partly to blame—in the Midwest, the sailboat-racing season is a short one.

* * * * *

There were binges of sailing and of drinking.

The night practice before the race the next weekend was set for 6:00 p.m., summer, the lake exploding in light of thousand shimmers. The air hot from the sun made gentler by the breeze from the lake. A perfect morning promising to turn into a perfect day.

I was packing the cooler. Carefully, as if it was full of baby chicks, I arranged the bottles, the icepacks. This was the most important aspect of the day—not that I would ever admit to that. I would admit to the important parts being contacting the crew members to confirm their attendance at practice or chasing down boat parts if repairs needed to be made.

As the day went on, I practically shook with anticipation. I could feel the blood coursing through my body faster, heart already switching to the next gear, the adrenaline making me lightheaded.

Back then, I loved nothing more than to be close to danger. I didn't admit this to myself—I thought of myself as cautious—but in retrospect, that's what made me feel most alive. It was one of those things where my own self was at war with myself—I was craving safety and I was scared of living without the buffer of oblivion. One more thing to keep me away from reality, from realizing that I could die if I rushed through life at this maddening pace.

Did I have a death wish? I don't know. Not consciously. I was filled with joy for life.

Yet, there I was—a walking paradox, ready to slice the water with my sailboat at a demon speed, aware of every injury that could occur and not being able to let my cautious nature override my excitement about it all.

The boat would launch at 5:30. We'd practice for an hour, in perfect unison. My whole body and thoughts were filled with the upcoming adventure.

I was doing what I love best. Yet, in the back of my mind, the reptilian part of the brain, there was a hiss. Cold, amber waterfall over ice cubes. The taste, the warmth spreading inside—it was a physical memory and it was torture to experience it as a fantasy only.

I told myself to pay attention to the boat, but once I acknowledged the fantasy, my mind would split over all the hissing, the hiss of alcohol, the hiss of water against the boat.

Imagine going on a date with the woman of your dreams and all you can think about is a TV show you're going to miss.

Imagine driving a Ferrari and obsessing over answering the text that just came through.

Imagine galloping on a horse through meadows and all you can think of are the new cushions you need to buy for your couch.

Imagine…

I imagined the drink and I couldn't stop imagining it, so when the fantasy finally materialized itself, I chugged down the whole delicious bottle to the sound of friends joking and talking about the practice. I, too, had things to say, and I would say them shortly; I just needed to get this drink down first, open myself properly, and then jump into the conversation.

There was a lot of back-slapping. We were having so much fun. Everything was a little too fast, like the sailing, but that was the spirit of the evening.

We would go to the restaurant across the street from the yacht club, where we were treated like royalty, like rockstars, with a metaphorical red carpet rolled out for us as we spent more on drinks than food and left a pile of money at the end of the night. Four or five hours of drinking and dining and laughing, and more slapping on the back again, and I was overwhelmed with our camaraderie.

I've never been this happy in my life! My head was spinning from this happiness and I thought that I'd absolutely need to repeat this—and I would repeat it—over and over. In fact, that night was exactly like the movie *Groundhog Day*: it was just a repeat of dozens of nights like it before.

I didn't like to think about what would happen later, in the morning. Only the moment mattered. I was—and am—a guy for whom the moment is the only time that matters.

Back at the restaurant, a distressing thing would start to happen. My friends would begin to disperse. One at a time. But then eventually, I was left on my own. It was Tuesday. Or a night like a Tuesday. A middle-of-the-week night.

Some friends have joked before that I must've had some kind of special powers to keep them out that late on a school night.

I sure do have special powers, I thought in my blitzed-out brain.

Occasionally, I was able to manage to talk my friends into staying longer. It depended on how mad their wives were at me at the time.

As the night went on, eventually, the restaurant would get in the way of my drinking, insisting on closing itself and forcing me to drive home.

I drove in silence, angry at the restaurant but happy about my loyal, best friends.

By the time I arrived home, my family was in bed, asleep. Good.

I was thirsty after my long drive. There was never such a thing as enough. My mind, albeit barely functioning, was unable to quiet in such silence, without company to distract it. There was only one thing I could do about it. I would mix a drink and head down to my office to turn on the TV.

I couldn't really see what was on TV. Voices and heads talking and laughing. It was an artificial re-creation of the evening I've just had. Now, I didn't feel so alone; the silence was defeated. I laughed at some joke someone said on TV. Or did he say a joke? It didn't matter; it was funny.

Then I felt terrible. I thought about my wife upstairs in bed, alone. I almost felt like crying.

I cried.

I stopped crying.

Everything was fine.

It was a great evening. I had a drink in my hand. I had a few more drinks.

I almost never allowed myself to pass out in the basement.

With great effort and blurred emotional pain, I forced myself to put down the glass.

I stumbled through the house the way I had done so many other times before. I somehow always managed to find the stairs. I walked slowly, tiptoeing, as if that would make a difference. As if that would convince anybody—who? Myself?—that I was anything but completely plastered.

I would crash into the bed, beside my wife, like a drunken, clumsy bear.

In the morning, the smell of booze coming out of my pores was so strong that even I could smell it.

My wife was awake. My wife's eyes were tired, sad. She was silent but she didn't have to say anything.

I wished for her to go away, to let me stay in bed with this head that seemed to be filled with rocks and seesaws. There was tightness in my chest. Anxiety so overwhelming that for a moment or two I thought how much better it would be if I were dead.

I dragged myself to the shower.

Have you ever been afraid to look in the mirror? It's a human instinct to glance in any reflecting surface. From our beginnings as babies, it's a natural curiosity, this need of confirmation of our existence by looking at ourselves. But I didn't want to confirm my existence.

I brushed my teeth, gargled half a bottle of Scope. I scrubbed myself as if I had rolled around in excrement the night before, which I had, in a way. I couldn't afford to smell like booze all day.

Twenty-minute scrub. Head to toe.

It was like Lady Macbeth trying to wash her hands of invisible blood spots. I could still smell it even though I'm sure I've washed out every single molecule of that damned scent, an evidence of me murdering myself.

There were moans, too. I didn't understand where they were coming from at first. It sounded like some wounded animal.

The moans were coming from me. I was moaning. Not just from the pain and discomfort of the crushing hangover.

I was moaning from feeling hopeless. I felt so alone. Again.

I could stay in this shower for hours, I thought. I didn't want to leave the bathroom. I didn't want to see my wife's sad, reproachful eyes or my children who knew too—children know things. Why wouldn't they hate me, too?

I didn't want to be surrounded by hate, yet I brought it all on myself. My children were not hateful people and neither was my wife, so it wasn't like I was basing this on some kind of evidence, but I was projecting. And I hated me.

The thing on the wall. I still managed to avoid it. It was like a black hole trying to suck me in: look, look, look!

I finally looked. I don't know what I was expecting to see there. The monster that lived inside me?

My eyes. The colors of the American flag. Blue pupils, red whites. I was a monster. The mirror didn't lie. I stood in front of it and stared. The self-loathing was now engulfing me in its flames finitely.

Why do I do this? What's wrong with me?

I could see nothing inside those eyes. Just emptiness. I wasn't even there. Where was I? Who was I?

Everything I felt now confirmed what I've always believed: I didn't belong. I was a mistake. I was a mistake to myself.

I poured Visine into my eyes until I had finally washed out all the red.

I looked at my face, and it was puffy, bright red, as though the alcohol vapor was catching fire as it jetted from my pores.

How would I make it through the day, given how I felt? The actual race was on later on; I couldn't imagine even making it to the shore. It was ridiculous. There was no way I was going to be able to pull it off.

I was convinced I would have a heart attack any moment now. And if not my heart, then my liver would explode, my guts. It felt as if something inside me was broken or was in the process of breaking—not just emotionally but physically, too. I had to stop drinking.

How could I stop drinking? Stopping drinking would mean facing myself in the mirror every day. No buffers. Just reality, clear and simple. No running away from it, from myself, from anything.

And the sad, abandoned bastard in my head? He'd just scream louder and louder that *I am worth nothing,* that *I am a piece of shit.* I've been able to quiet him down, here and there, with booze; get him so drunk he'd pass out. But sober, he would be back and I was sure he would drive me to madness.

But what was this if not madness? This standing in front of the mirror and looking at myself and feeling like a soulless monster? This was precisely what monsters did—destroyed their lives, their loved ones' lives.

I dragged myself away from the mirror. I opened the door to the sun-dappled house.

"Hello!"

My greeting was fake-happy. Too strained. And I was right. They could tell right away. Our miseries reflected in each other's eyes.

"How's everybody doing?" I said in a voice that could replace a cheerleading squad.

"Great, Dad, great. How are you?"

"I'm great! I'm great!"

"That's good," said Vicki, a note of strain in her voice; the "good" was flat. "We're done with breakfast so I've got to take the kids to the club," she said.

I was happy to be left alone. I could moan in peace. I wouldn't have them around me, witnessing my overwhelming Shame. My self-loathing.

They knew I was not as I was pretending to be. They knew I was a hypocrite: a man professing that his family was the most important thing in the world, but drinking his face off at the yacht club instead of spending time at home with them. They probably disliked me as much as I disliked myself. How could they feel otherwise?

* * * * *

You overreacted. Look. What a beautiful day. Look at this lake. Look at Piranha; how much stronger and more beautiful she looks compared to other scows. Look at your wife, she's not mad at you at all, now! She's waving and smiling! And your family has been helping you all day to get all the other family members and spare sails and parts to the race…Why did you ever think they hated you?!

My brain was back to its jovial, pre-drunk mode. It talked bullshit at me and I bought it because it was easy. More delusion, and delusion was where it was most comfortable for me.

The bullshit was working. I was stronger, healthier; my head was no longer a bag of rocks. I didn't think I was really that bad. Okay, so I had overdone it the night before, so what? *I'll take it easy tonight*, I thought to myself and opened the first beer of the day.

I watched my wife get ready for the "Beverage Dispersal," which is where she and other wives would throw us cold beers at the finish line. I was cheered by the thought: she couldn't have had been that upset at me before if she was okay with this part of the ceremony. Obviously. I imagined it all.

I was starting to feel better about everything now. I was not a monster. I was a fun guy, a great athlete and people loved me. I felt there was a need for celebration — of that, of the fact that I was so fortunate. A celebration of life. Life was so short. I needed to up this feeling of joy. Make it euphoric. I would take this feeling as high as I could. I knew what to do to achieve that.

* * * * *

By the time I finished my first drink at the yacht club after the race, I was completely reacquainted with the belief that things were perfectly fine the way they were.

By the second drink, I was convinced of it.

By the 12th, my family had gone home, and most of my teammates had left with their families.

Why was I still at the bar? Alone? Like the night before? Exactly like the night before. Everyone had abandoned me. What kind of friends…?

It was time to go home, too. The bar staff were polite but I could tell they were tired and wanted to leave. Ungrateful. All those tips. My friends, too. Ungrateful. If they didn't care about me, there was nothing I could do. My joy was gone, now. There was instead intense, desperate sorrow. A grown man crying—pathetic. And I cried the night before and now, again. Loser.

But nobody could see my tears in the darkness as I stumbled toward the boat with two drinks for the road, my only companions who didn't abandon me.

I putted very slowly along the shore. I drank my drinks. The lake reflected the moon and it was beautiful, unearthly. I felt something distant and beautiful and unearthly within myself, too. A sensation, I wouldn't be able to name until later. A oneness with nature, the knowledge of being accepted and held as if in mother's arms. The feeling was, however, faint and muddied by my drunkenness.

Too bad.

Whatever, I didn't care. And like that, the sensation disappeared. There was no oneness. There was only loneliness.

By the time I got home, *Groundhog Day* again, I could no longer keep away the dread and doom that was flooding over me. There wasn't much to look forward to. Maybe next Tuesday night's practice. Some adventures in the future. But right now? Nothing.

My family was asleep again. I poured myself a drink so tall it was more like a pitcher. I slithered down to my basement office.

There was some relief now, the dread still present, but at least I was going somewhere familiar. Somewhere special. My couch. The A & E show *Intervention* was going to be on shortly. Those poor folks! I was nothing like them. They had it really bad. I was so glad I wasn't like them. I was troubled, but I was not at all like the junkies yelling at their parents, the ugly drunks drinking out of jars, the Meth-addicted woman breaking her baby sister's piggy bank to steal all the pennies to buy drugs.

It suddenly occurred to me that I might have to get a new TV. The pictures on the screen were blurry; there was something wrong with the volume. I didn't want to turn it up for the fear of waking up my family.

There was something wrong with the glass of drink, too; it was defective. It was now empty. Did I spill it or did I drink it? I tried getting up but I was defective, too; I couldn't move. Might as well just stay where I was. Close my eyes. Some fleeting thought about never doing this again.

And I would do it again.

And again.

And again.

And again.

And again.

* * * * *

But, no! I wasn't an alcoholic. I really wasn't.

Or was I? I couldn't tell myself that yet, and I couldn't tell anybody else that. I didn't know how to be without alcohol—it was the only thing in the world that would mute all the noise in my head, all the horrible things I thought about myself: an adoptee, unwanted, embarrassing, hateful. A person full of Shame. And, finally, a drunk.

It was like with the Drunkard in *The Little Prince*:

"I am drinking," replied the Drunkard, with a lugubrious air.

"Why are you drinking?" demanded the Little Prince.

"So that I may forget," replied the Drunkard.

"Forget what?" inquired the Little Prince, who already was sorry for him.

"Forget that I am ashamed," the Drunkard confessed, hanging his head.

"Ashamed of what?" insisted the Little Prince, who wanted to help him.

"Ashamed of drinking!" The Drunkard brought his speech to an end, and shut himself up in an impregnable silence.

(From *The Little Prince* by Antoine de Saint-Exupéry)

More Fun

One of the biggest luxuries, thanks to my retirement fund, was the ability to take lots of wonderful family vacations. Skiing in Colorado. Sailing in the British Virgin Islands, from island to island, exploring, laughing, feeling joy pumping in our veins as we looked out onto the azure and then the dark blue of the horizon ahead of us. My heart beating in my ears, so thirsty the whole time—for new adventures, for more of everything.

Arriving at the impossibly beautiful Virgin Gorda boulders, massive like houses—some of which were stacked over the shallow waters forming a sort of a roof over you. The sun filtering through the top of the formations, hitting the crystal-clear water in the rainbow spectrum of light. It was like nature's cathedral. It took your breath away. It almost took my breath away, but I was busy, elsewhere in my head. I was looking at my watch: *Two hours to go, two more hours, what a beautiful sight, I've never seen anything like this before, two more hours.*

What did this place look like when the ocean rages on? During a storm? It would be terrifying, like something out of Greek mythology—gods fighting with each other—thunders and roaring water; Poseidon with his trident pointing at the waves, smashing them hard against the rocks.

"David!" My wife, so beautiful still—always—the same girl I met decades ago on a beach, the same girl I fell in love with when the sun hit her skin covered in droplets of water. It was the same now, even after all these years. She still sparkled, her smile was the same. She was pointing a camera at me. Our children, Andrew and Adrienne, looking at something in the sand, a starfish or a shell; it was hard to tell from where I was standing.

"David!"

David, David. It was getting too hot. *How many hours can one man stand in the sun? This is unbearable.*

Two more hours? Or one more hour? No, two more. Let's make it to 4 p.m. Look at that rock! What a giant rock—what would be like to climb it? Climb it! Go for it! Don't do it. Two more hours. Less than two hours now. Look at the watch. One hour and 55 minutes. Less than two hours. My brain was shouting at me as usual. My inner life completely out of sync with whatever was happening around me.

I felt nervous. Not about the rock. I didn't know why I felt nervous. I knew why I felt nervous. Yes, I knew, but I couldn't name it. I just felt it. A giant hole opening inside me ready to swallow me and the ocean and my wife and my children. It was bigger than any of these stupid boulders; it was bigger than anything in this world.

I imagined my hands were shaking, but they weren't when I looked down at them. So what was shaking? It felt like some kind of a current running through my body that I couldn't even see, but it was there and my thoughts were racing along with it, *What was going on? What was going to happen? Let's leave here! Let's go, let's go.*

I clenched my jaw. *Make it stop.*

My children ran up to me. They smelled of the ocean, the sun. Their faces were covered in freckles. They were beautiful. I smiled at them and they smiled back: *Look how happy Dad is!*

I said nothing. I looked at my wife. She snapped a photo of me with my arms around our beautiful children; my boy almost as tall as me, my daughter now my height.

We appear so relaxed in those pictures.

But I know that inside me there was a storm. The thoughts were racing, crashing like waves against the boulders, as the camera went off. At 4 p.m. I could have a cocktail—the rum here was the best in the world. It would be ridiculous not to drink it. When in Rome…

Well, I went to Rome once. Never mind.

* * * * *

By 9:00 p.m. I would be alone, on the deck, my thoughts quieting down, the ocean unpredictable but right now pretending to be calm, all quiet and black, its vastness opened right before me.

I knew it was an illusion; the ocean's quiet was. Whenever I was by the ocean now, I couldn't help but think about one crazy trip I went on, one year into my retirement. My brother-in-law talked me into helping bring his new yacht from England to Gibraltar. It sounded like a great adventure. I pictured myself like some kind of a character from a book or from a movie, powering through the water, standing majestically at the tip of the boat, my hair getting playfully tousled by the wind.

We sailed for 11 days and 11 nights and it was a pure nightmare, beyond anything we'd imagined. There was almost no hour when I didn't feel my life endangered by everything that was going on around us. Waves, wind, rain…a whirlwind of atmospheric calamities. The big, solid yacht would turn into a little, wimpy paper boat from one moment to the next. We were completely at the mercy of the ocean. Sure, one expects some rain and waves but this was something else. This was a hellish roller-coaster. We took turns to steer and sleep and eat, but the schedule was strict, almost no wiggle room, one-hour to two-hour intervals because there was no way we could afford to ever let our guard down. The waves would get us.

But there was one moment. A big moment. It happened one night when the waves quieted down and the sailing was smoother. We were exhausted. The yacht was way off shore, and the only lights we could see were of cargo ships crisscrossing the international shipping lanes. I lay down and stared at the sky. Every-thing seemed to stand still. The sky above me connected to the water; there seemed to be no limit to either—the stars or the ocean.

I felt an incredible and deep peace, some kind of a primal sensation that every human must be born with—the understanding that I wasn't, after all, alone. It was as if I was swaddled by the world. No money, no ad-venture, no alcohol could make me feel connected to it in the way that I wanted to connect, but in that one moment, I felt truly a part of everything.

There's a psychological term coined by a Nobel-prize winner novelist Romain Rolland, called "oceanic feeling." According to the definition, "This feeling is the source of all religious energy which per-meates in various religious systems. It is a sensation of an indissoluble bond, as of being connected with the external world in its integral form."

I was never a religious guy, but that was one time I felt spirituality rushing right through me.

Incidentally, years later, I also questioned if what happened was my simply coming out of a grand-mal sei-zure. All the worries and the crashing waves wiped out by my tortured doings.

* * * * *

Back in the Caribbean, on my family vacations, with a bottle of the finest rum right beside me, looking at the ocean, I tried to search for that connection, that feeling, but I could never find it again.

Or perhaps I was too wasted to notice it anyway.

* * * * *

At home, the social times started to slowly come to a halt when it became clear to many people around me that I was at the epicenter of all the great fun that was starting to affect some of my friends' lives.

I was the only one who didn't have to get up the next day—although I tried to, to be there for my kids—so I became the slippery guy, the party guy your wife didn't want you to hang out with on Tuesday and Wednesday and Thursday and Monday. She didn't want you to hang out with me because you had to go to work the next day. I became the guy you wanted to avoid.

People started to cancel on me. I was still able to find drinking buddies, but there were fewer and fewer. That was fine. I didn't need them. I was okay on my own. Who needs friends like that in the first place? You do things for them, you take them out, you pay for everything and they don't even have an evening to spare to hang out with you?

It never occurred to me that alcohol was the only glue that kept so many of those friendships together.

The Box Reopened

Remember the box? There was a box. Or there was about to be a box.

First, there was blackness, an abyss. There was a seizure, emergency technicians around my bed, my wife's worried eyes, as I came to. I was in my own home, but I couldn't quite register that or anything else, in fact. Not even words that were coming at me, people asking me what date it was, where I was, what my name was.

What is my name? But that is ridiculous! My name is —

And there would be a blank space and letters trying to form into a word.

"What is your name?"

My name — I couldn't get it out.

What happened? I didn't understand any of this. I couldn't ask either — my mouth hurt like a wound.

"You had a seizure, David," —*David, that's my name!* —my wife said.

A seizure?

"Don't move," a paramedic advised. They were taking my vitals.

"Do you know what happened?" another paramedic asked. Why would he ask me that? I was just told what happened. Did they think I was brain damaged?

What happened?

I had a seizure.

"What year is it?"

"It's 2004," I was finally able to speak.

"What month?"

"January."

There was a ski trip recently. I recalled my wife and my kids' big smiles, their red cheeks. The perfect snow, not too powdery, not too wet. And after a few rounds, finally, a nice tumbler of liquid amber—a reward after such a busy, productive time. It was a reward. I wasn't doing splendidly well after a recent physical injury. But occasionally, I managed to conjure the old me, schussing down the hill like I was still a kid.

"January, good. January what?"

"January 4th."

My body was so sore. It felt as if someone had beaten me up, or tried to pull me apart. Every muscle was strained, exhausted. My tongue seemed shredded; I had bitten it repeatedly while seizing.

I was terrified. It was terrifying to not have control over my own body; it was as if my body had a mind of its own and it wasn't my mind. Whose mind was it? Ridiculous. I liked to be in charge of things. I planned, executed, recovered.

"Has this happened before?"

"Once," I said. Once that was documented. But now I thought back to the crazy sailing trip to Gibraltar. Me looking at the sky, feeling swaddled, time standing still. Oceanic feeling or grand mal seizure/

So twice? Maybe more. Maybe there were other times. How is a drunk supposed to know those things? Things that require utmost attention in the best circumstances.

Control. I had no control. No such thing. How many blackouts? How many surprising remains of the night before: emails sent out without recollection, notes that made no sense, plans made and forgotten.

I was only aware of one official seizure, so I said once.

That was still enough to get everyone more alarmed than they needed to be. I was going to be fine.

"I'm going to be fine."

"You're not fine, David," Vicki said later. "We need to get you checked out."

She was right. There was some relief in hearing her say that, in disagreeing with me. Sometimes it was nice to not have to carry the burden of…myself. I was a burden. I couldn't handle myself. I knew we were only talking about my seizure, but there were so many other things I desperately wanted to get checked out, despite seemingly not wanting to know, I wanted to know everything about myself, why I was the way I was. There were a lot of things in my life that I was ashamed of, and I knew that Shame was already a massive, invisible monster permanently attached to me, dragging me with it or my dragging it—whichever. The point is we belonged to one another.

"You're not fine."

"No, I'm not fine," I said to Vicki. "I will get tested. We'll figure this out."

* * * * *

This is how I arrived at the mysterious box.

One common quality of addicts is that addicts are incapable of facing the reality of the addiction. But it's not just *that* reality. It is reality in general. Something happens and an addict crumbles, can no longer face it— addiction sneaks in, sometimes it stays.

Sometimes it stays for a long time, for a lifetime even.

With the combination of genetics and environmental factors, there are those of us who are predisposed to addiction more so than others. It's a little bit like with the show *Intervention*, at one point my constant companion as I drank myself to death in my basement office. It follows the same story formula; it's set up in a way that it usually pinpoints one significant event as an offset of hell. Whether it's a divorce of parents, an assault, the death of a loved one—any kind of event that shakes a person to the core. Something happens in an addict's life that makes him or her incapable of functioning in reality the way a non-addict does. But that's just for television. It's scripted even though it's supposed to show the reality of addiction.

Life…it's not as simple. No script. Sometimes there are many reasons for addiction, justifiable reasons, however you define those. But other times, it might seem like it's nothing, just dumb luck or lack of it; you drink socially for years and years only to develop addiction later in life as it sneaks up on you, completely unexpected.

Sometimes, it's something that wouldn't make one as much as blink, but it will be severely traumatic to someone else with a different kind of disposition. Telling my friends that I was adopted and subsequently feeling Shame about that fact was enough to make me doubt my entire existence. It didn't make me drink or use right away—I was only a child—but from that one particular moment on, it was as if I was no longer anchored to the ground. No matter how attentive and loving my adoptive parents were, how popular I was at school, how successful at work—I was never able to quite land. I floated.

When my daughter was born and I saw myself in her, and when my son was born and I saw even more of me in him, were two moments I knew I belonged on this planet, but those moments, despite their gravity, were not enough to conquer years of doubt and heartache. The only thing that made me feel temporarily *here* was alcohol, however artificially that feeling was created. I felt it in camaraderie of other drunks; I felt it in the golden flow of it in my veins. Easy. Ease and comfort. Don't have to think, don't have to feel anything.

I could do something about it tomorrow—there was always tomorrow, always a chance to reinvent myself to change. There was no rush.

Now there was rush. There was urgency.

Now, with the seizure and the questions about its origins, I had to face certain truths. If I didn't, I would die.

Something in my genetic makeup caused the epilepsy. It wasn't the alcohol or painkillers that I was taking. The doctors listened politely and prescribed Topamax, which gave me hangovers from hell and was supposed to stave off my cravings.

I had to hand in my medical history. To be more specific, I had to discover my history before I became a son of a dark-haired beauty named Joan. Long before that. Before I was even born. I had to discover *her* history. Karen's. My biological mother.

* * * * *

And that's how the box happened. Inside it, the facts: Miss Karen Bender, 56 years old, died in 1996 of alcoholism. The red-headed coed, the flight attendant, a mother to three daughters and two sons—one, me, relinquished— and, eventually, a ghost of herself dying slowly in a heap of old blankets in a rented storage locker. Then her final hour in a homeless shelter, her lonely, tragic heart seizing in her chest. Alone, isolated like a sick, dying animal, hiding from the world. Not wanting to bother anyone. No one around to see her final departure.

Was it me who was the catalyst? At the time, when I found out her name, it was too much to think about. I didn't know about her tragic death then either. All I had was some basic information: "Baby Boy Bender" on the birth certificate. That last name, a grand irony or what?

I knew that relatives said she died of alcoholism. At the time I *still* wasn't using the word "alcoholic" in reference to myself, even though I thought I was drinking myself to death. My heart was pounding in my chest, I was brushing my teeth three times to disguise the smell of booze, I was waking up with a thunderous headache–yet I was *not* an alcoholic.

When I read that my biological mother had died of alcoholism, I didn't want to know what that looked like, so I locked everything in a box. I couldn't deal with any of it anyway. It was my own Schröding-er's Cat experiment, the cat both dead and alive. My reality and my unreality. A totally abstract past I had nothing to do with, but that made up who I was. The past that held the answer to all the questions—or at least the questions that never had answers. I knew what was in the box, but I was in too much denial to acknowledge the box, even though I had put it up on the shelf myself. The progression of my alcoholism went off the charts.

Broken Hearts

There's a term used in the rooms of 12-step fellow-ships that dismissively describes the stories that alcoholics tell: "drunk-a-log." These are stories that specifically talk about things that happened during drinking, such as my recollections of slamming into my friend's car on New Year's Eve, drinking myself out of college, or going on a bender at the Vatican. These are not stories of "recovery"— supposedly no wisdom to share there. That comes later after you get enough experience.

Does this mean that "drunk-a-log" stories are worthless? Self-indulgent?

Absolutely not.

There's value in every story.

It's wrong to dismiss stories of alcoholics who un-pack their addictions. The word "drunk-a-log" implies that the stories aren't that important, that telling of them is nothing but only droning on.

"Just tell us how you got sober. We don't need to hear all the crazy stuff. We've all been there," some long-time members ("old-timers") in recovery might say. One example of how badly things have gotten should be enough. No need to go on. Nonsense. We are not *just* recovery. We are composed of stories, good and bad. They are as much part of us as is our human DNA. From our prehistoric beginnings with primitive etchings on walls to our over-sharing of the Internet age, people constantly exchange information about themselves, and tales about drinking are as important as any other information about what it is to be human.

Addiction is possibly one of the most baffling human conditions. The more we talk about it—all aspects of it—the closer we are to understanding it. We might never understand it fully, but we need to mull it over and over—expose ourselves and others to it, make it so common that it no longer scares us and others, no longer stigmatizes those who need help. People have to be able to relate, and even if you haven't had a chance to drop a few thousand dollars in Vatican City, a bender is still a bender.

We also tell stories because they help us put things in context. Without stories, all we have left are events and feelings that are completely meaningless on their own, because where and how do they belong?

How is it that a 45-year-old, successful man loved by so many people—his family, his friends—spends most of his evenings drinking himself into oblivion in a basement office? Why is he having a seizure in his bed, next to his wife? Why is he putting the information about his family history away in a box to avoid confronting the reality?

An event, a feeling, a situation that might mark a crucial point in someone's life, without context, the point will be simply lost. And even once there is a point and it's clearer because of the context, there's no guarantee that that will lead anywhere anyway. Wisdom is the best you can hope for. Wisdom is the best you can get. Wisdom is wanting more but understanding the limits. Life is not a Disney movie; there are many layers, many parallels.

The final days of my drinking were the opposite of wisdom, although seen now, the events simply reveal themselves as a succession of bottoms that led me to my final drink.

* * * * *

Sometimes, the bigger the problem, the more grandiose the bottom. My drinking problem became so big that it almost stopped a plane. I was going to visit my daughter in Florida for a four-day-long weekend.

At that point in my life, everyone around me had learned how to adjust themselves to my drinking. This is what an addict does; he forces other people to change. He doesn't change, but people around him have to make room for the addiction. And in my case, that meant that no one was ever sure about what kind of David they would get. Everyone was walking around me on the proverbial eggshells. I was aware of it and it added to my ongoing Shame. So that weekend I needed to rectify it. At least a little bit. I wanted to be sober for my daughter. I wanted her to have a nice, relaxing weekend with her dad. I did not drink that day before the flight.

That is probably why, when I got on the plane, I started to go into a withdrawal.

I felt it coming on, ten minutes after the plane took off. I couldn't tell what was happening, but it seemed massive and scary, and there seemed nothing I was going to be able to do about it.

I felt claustrophobic, there was not enough room, not enough air. I was too big for the plane. At the same time, I was suddenly aware of the plane being just a small metal speck in the air, and me so big on it a second ago, but now the size of a bacteria. The two feelings—I'm too big; I'm too small—fought inside my withdrawal brain as I tried to sit and wait it out. But there was no waiting it out. The flight attendant must have noticed there was something wrong because she stopped and asked me how I was feeling.

I'm dying. I'm dying. I need to get out, I need to go, I thought.

Out loud, I said I wasn't feeling great. But it was probably going to pass. Then a thought occurred to me: *What if this is a heart attack?* I corrected my answer, "I think I'm really sick."

I was given oxygen. I tried to suck more out of the container than was in there. I took big gulps but nothing was helping. I wanted to jump out of my skin.

Get me off the plane, I said or thought. I wasn't sure which.

The flight attendant said, "Is there anything else I can get you?"

"A really tall Jack Daniels on the rocks."

Her eyes big and kind on me. In that instant, I knew that she knew. She could probably smell it on me anyway. There was pity in her smile. I didn't want her to look at me that way. I wanted to look away. I wanted my Jack Daniels on the rocks. It would help. If she could only...

"I'm going to talk to the pilot," she said.

I heaved and sweated. I was going to die.

She came back, "We're going to divert to Kansas City. We'll get you in an ambulance."

God, now what? What was she talking about? No. Absolutely not.

I looked around. I realized then that I was making a spectacle. What I thought was a quiet conversation between me and the flight attendant was broadcast to the whole section of the plane. There weren't a lot of people in first class where I was, but now I noticed all the eyes on me. Angry eyes. Not like hers, full of pity. The plane was going to get diverted? No, absolutely not. I felt terrible enough. Not this humiliation. I couldn't let it happen.

I begged the flight attendant to plead with the pilot. I would make it to Tampa. They could call an ambulance there. It was just an anxiety attack. "I've had one before," I said. I tried to look healthier. I wasn't sure how to do that, so I sat up straight in my chair, but I felt so nauseous that I slumped back into my discomfort immediately.

The paramedics were like the flight attendant. I knew they knew. They took my vitals. I avoided eyes this time.

I will not drink on this trip. I will not drink on this trip.

* * * * *

My daughter looked beautiful and healthy. I didn't. My clothes were crumpled. I was sweating. I knew that she knew. But we were good at this game: alcoholic dad, daughter of an alcoholic dad. Neither of us said anything.

"Just an anxiety attack. Nothing to worry about it. I'll have it checked out," I promised her.

"Okay, Dad. Whatever you say, Dad." This said tenderly, not rudely. Such a distinct note of sadness in her voice. Barely there but so loud, echoing inside me for years to come. Even now I hear it.

On the third day of my stay, I got a prescription for Ativan at a walk-in clinic. I flew back home in a benzo Nirvana.

After getting back, I was very careful about the Ativan. I threw the pills away as soon as I realized I was getting high on them. I did not judge my use of alcohol in the same way; I still wasn't entirely sure that it was a problem. All the evidence pointed to it, but I would have to think about it some other time. Not then, not yet.

After I got sober, I never had another panic attack.

* * * * *

The final story of my drunk-a-log is how I beat the odds. I lived past my expiration date. At the time, I didn't know it. Only years later the death of my biological mother was described to me in detail, and I now understood that my sobriety was nothing short of a glitch in the natural order of things—my genetic legacy of dying drunk. A curse almost as real as the red hair I had inherited from Karen.

* * * * *

The last time Karen drank, she phoned her ex-husband. She did that, phoned men she knew, to ask them for favors. At 56, she was still attractive despite having been ravaged by alcohol. There was faded beauty to her. The way everything that was in her was faded now, long gone, almost dead. Her body still functioned, but barely. It sustained itself on vodka; it propelled itself forward on that gasoline.

She asked her ex-husband to drop her off at an apartment building where she said she lived.

* * * * *

The last time I drank, I was alone. I had just come back from a sailing event. For some reason I didn't want to be at the event. For the first time ever, I wanted to escape all that fun, go home.

At the event, I drank for six hours, yet I couldn't get drunk. I drove home. My wife had left for Florida; my son was gone to a football practice with his friends.

It was 9:30 in the morning. I started drinking again. There was a feeling of inevitability. I never drank that early in the day. A friend came over and it was the same thing with the eyes, the same kind of pity I was now so getting used to seeing.

"I'm fine, I'm fine," I slurred.

"Is there anything I can do to help you?"

"I'm fine."

The friend left.

I went back to drinking.

In my basement, I sat at my desk. And drank. And drank.

* * * * *

They didn't know how Karen ended up in a homeless shelter. But that's where she died. Massive heart attack in a room by herself. No one there. Not a soul. Her last breath. Did she fight for it or did she give it away with relief? Would there finally be peace after the tragedy that was her life? Nobody knew. Nobody knew much. After her death, her last hours were traced to the apartment building where she had asked to get dropped off. Nobody in the building knew who she was.

But some information was unearthed: she owned a storage unit.

The only things in the storage unit were dirty blankets, two empty quarts of vodka, and a receipt from the liquor store from the night before she died.

* * * * *

Hers is a story that needed telling. Hers is a story that puts my own life into context. The life I am living now is one of a survivor of his own legacy, the happiest freak of nature there ever was who has to constantly check in with reality to make sure he doesn't end up like Karen. Hers wasn't a heart attack. It was her heart that broke. Mine would repair.

My Name Is David

My family was away the night I drank too much and fell into unconsciousness in the basement. I believe I was in a blackout and although I wasn't dead, I might as well have been. Blackout is a type of death; you check out with no recollection, there are no flashbacks, nothing.

When I came to and listened to my messages later, there were dozens of them from concerned family members. People were trying to reach me, get me to wake up, come out of my blackout.

I called my wife. "I can't do this anymore," I said. My voice broke into a sob. Do what? I wasn't even sure I meant drinking. I just meant *everything*.

Everything I was doing: living in those Parallel Universes: the supposedly sane, sober one and the drunk one; the one where I looked like everything was okay, and the one where everything crumbled. The ghost of me as a grown-up Baby Boy Bender and me, David.

I cried loudly, cathartically, all the lies washing out of me as my wife waited patiently on the other side of the phone.

I didn't want to be alone. I wanted to be with her and with my son and my daughter. I wanted to have a normal life, just *one* life. Just the one I was pretending to be having. It was so exhausting to carry on the way I was. It wasn't fun anymore. I wasn't sure when the fun stopped, but it had a long time ago. Every single thing I did now revolved around alcohol. I was either waiting to be able to be with it again—under the disguise of a party, a sailing event, business research in the basement—or I was with it…or I was passed out.

"What are you planning to do?" my wife sighed.

I didn't expect her to be warm. In fact, she had every reason to hang up on me. But she didn't. We talked about my plans. I would call a help line. I would go for an assessment, confess to my drinking, get sober.

After we finished talking, I called the help line. They scheduled me for an assessment to see if I was an alcoholic. I would possibly be going to treatment.

I was determined but I was scared. What will the treatment involve? Shock therapy? Will I be strapped to bed? It didn't matter. I was committed to doing whatever it would take. There was only one problem.

I didn't need an assessment.

I was an alcoholic.

I phoned them back.

"I'm an alcoholic," I said. "I don't need an assessment. Just take me in."

And they did.

* * * * *

I love reading addiction memoirs. To date, I've read dozens and dozens of addictions memoirs — the famous ones of Christiane F. (*We Children of Bahnhof Zoo*) and Jerry Stahl (*Permanent Midnight*), and the less famous ones. The ones with blood spilling all over the place from needles, with bug-infested mattresses, matted hair, screaming babies, overdoses. With degradation so heartbreaking that it seemed impossible for the author to be able to ever get back into humanity. I read them partly to find myself in them, but I rarely could. At least on the surface, no one seemed like me. It didn't matter. When we escape our addictions, the desire to get sober is a desire to persevere, and that is the life force every human being is born with. The desperate junkie living on the street, the guy sailing boats with a house on the lake.

And once an addict digs himself out of the hot tar that is addiction, he will try anything to stay on the surface. Not all succeed. You can look up some of the famous memoirists and see for yourself how random a successful recovery seems to be. But when I read addiction memoirs, I relate to the "trying anything." Because that's what I had to do and that's what I did.

* * * * *

I immersed myself in recovery. From the moment I said I was an alcoholic and went to treatment, there was no looking back. I had no clue how I was going to forgo my parallel life of addiction and Shame, but I would have to do it in order to survive.

* * * * *

My admission to the treatment center had to be preceded by detox, and right away, things got more challenging than I thought they would be. One of the admitting doctors was the father of my son's friend. I was already lower than I had ever been, and seeing him approaching my wheelchair, I wanted to get up and run. I was beyond humiliated.

I waited.

I searched his face for judgment, a narrowing of the eyes, but there was only warmth, compassion.

"I'm glad you're here. I have people in my life who have this problem," he said, his hand resting on my shoulder.

I felt small and helpless, but as he was saying it, something happened. There *were* others. He—a doctor!—had people in his life who had the same problem. I wasn't a pariah. I needed help. This could work.

It was 4:00 a.m. I had left the house dressed as I was, no overnight bag, no change of clothes. I had to get to the hospital immediately.There was no room for debate, for waiting around. I was as extreme in my drive to become sober as I was in my drive to become drunker just few days prior.

"Thank you," I said to the doctor.

I was thanking him for giving me hope.

Later, I phoned my wife again, who phoned our son.

Andrew brought a bag of clothes to the hospital. He was the kindest he could possibly be, considering how much I'd scared him. I could see the look of pity and terror in his eyes.

"I'm really afraid for you, Dad," he said.

"I know. It's going to be okay," I said.

I was so ashamed. I was so relieved, too. I was so hungover. I was on anti-seizure drugs. This was my bottom. I saw it right there, in my son's eyes.

Sober Now

A few hours later, still hungover, feeling as fragile as a baby, I was in my first 12-step meeting.

I couldn't comprehend what was happening to me. The last 24 hours seemed like a half-nightmare, half-dream. All the walls around me were crumbling. Years of building a parallel life that I was so glad to be able to destroy completely, finally.

In the room full of strangers who looked nothing like me, I was about to open myself whole, make myself the most vulnerable I had been since that afternoon when I was a six-year-old kid revealing my adoptive status. The last time I felt truly authentic.

When it was my turn to say who I was, the words formed in my mouth and I said it: "My name is David and I'm an alcoholic."

Saying the words, admitting to who I was, gave me the relief that was bigger than Shame; the desire to stop drinking was genuine. It trumped Shame. This time— even though it wasn't the first time saying I was an alcoholic—felt profound, more emotional than anything I had experienced so far in the past 24 hours. Maybe because I've added my name to it—I signed under the verdict officially; the world now knew.

You're not an alcoholic, come on! A tiny voice squeaked inside me: a last-ditch attempt to double-speak to myself.

I am.

Oh, please, stop exaggerating. Look at those guys here. You're nothing like them. You're somebody. You've ac-complished things. You were just under a lot of stress. Anybody would—

My name is David and I'm an alcoholic, I repeated in my head. There was no doubt. The demon voice got weaker and weaker. Eventually it disappeared.

I looked at the gals and guys around me and I felt understood, recognized, even though it did seem we had nothing in common. Like with those addiction memoirs that were so dramatic, so unrelatable, it essen-tially didn't matter that these people were so different. We were at the treatment center because our addiction was making our lives impossible. A common cause or a reason. Whether it was my jet-setting life or the kind of life I was guessing a tattooed, bearded biker was hav-ing, no one was here because things were going well. We've all been to the same war. And when I said who I was, that was the truth. It was *my* Reality. And they understood that reality because they've lived it, too.

Immersing

A fter that first meeting, I sat in dozens of group sessions at the rehab facility, still full of skepticism, fear, confusion. Shame was sneaking its way back, but for now I immersed myself in my recovery.

In the sessions, I watched the people I dubbed COINS: Community of Individuals Needing Support— people who needed the same support I did. They were like coins because there were so many of them: they came from N.A., A.A., Marijuana Anonymous. There were also volunteers and professionals who talked about relapse prevention strategies, disease of addiction—finally, spirituality. I didn't always understand what was being taught, but I was determined. I had to adapt to survive. I was like a kid in kindergarten—wide-eyed, completely confused, eager to please, and terrified and excited.

I absorbed what was said in groups, what the counselors said to me, what was conveyed in the fellowship's literature.

I read the first 164 pages the first night at the treatment center.

This was my usual M.O., immersing myself completely in whatever I was passionate about. And what better thing to be passionate about than recovering? Not just recovering from alcoholism, but recovering your entire life.

I understood right away that this was no joke; I took rehab seriously. Not everyone did and there were moments I would get distracted by the chaos around me: fellow addicts sneaking out at night, making out in corridors, smoking, and even doing drugs. Different levels of motivation.

But I kept going, determined not to stop for one second to question my determination.

I was drained by all the teachings, and I was hungover that entire week, it seemed, but there was no other way. Once you decide to run a marathon, you have to finish it. If you're a guy like me. Incidentally, I was no longer a guy like me in that I had to shelve my aggressive, former trader self, the guy who was bent on being irreverent, bucking the trend, not making friends. I was out of my comfort zone, having been reduced to the wide-eyed kindergartner.

I was a lucky kindergartner. I found out in a counseling session with my wife that she had been going to leave me the day I phoned her and told her I was done. My timing was impeccable, she joked, after she berated me for an hour. I deserved more than an hour of that, I knew, and I cried with her because her kindness and strength were the things that made my recovery possible.

She joined a program for spouses of alcoholics three days after I became a member of a 12-step program. And if that isn't the ultimate support, I don't know what is. She had to be in a program because of something that I did, or, if I am to be kind to myself, because of something I was afflicted with. It didn't seem fair, but we both knew that that was going to be another pillar to make my sobriety more solid.

* * * * *

The stats are terrifying: one out of ten addicts is going to make it. I kept thinking, *I hope that's me, I hope that's me.*

I focused on me. I had to be protective of me.

Selfish? Not at all. Some of the teachings will tell you that 12- step programs are not selfish programs. One of their tenets is to spread the message of recovery to those who need it (Step 12: *"Having had a spiritual awakening as the result of these steps, we tried to carry this message to alcoholics, and to practice these principles in all our affairs."*).

But in the beginning, one must be so-called "selfish." And if you think about it, that selfishness will be exactly what will return you to your loved ones. That selfishness is what will make you selfless again where you will be productive and helpful and not a tragic, doomed addict hiding in the shadows.

I was told to find a sponsor, a person versed in recovery who would help me through my own recovery, take me through the steps and show me the way to live sober. I needed guidance. I needed a mentor.

There were guys coming in from the outside to put on the 12-step meetings, and I looked hungrily at each of them and tried to pick out the one who would suit me best. None of them would, I was realizing quickly. They were nothing like me. Blue-collar, rough, and most of them rode motorcycles as a lifestyle. But it didn't matter. This wasn't a dating service. We didn't have to have anything in common other than the way we drank and the fact that we were both bent on being sober.

* * * * *

Ronald had more than 25 years in recovery. He drove an 18-wheeler for a living. He had a long beard and rode a Harley on weekends. He was what is known as an old-timer, the kind of guy who would growl at you, "Shut up and listen." Or "Get rid of that ego thing you seem to have." Or "Take the cotton out of your ears and put it in your mouth."

For a man already so riddled with Shame, it was probably damaging to be humiliated in that way, but back then, I was willing to be put in place. I didn't stop to think if it was abusive, if my feelings were getting hurt. Yes, my feelings were getting hurt, but then I would hear another adage: "Feelings are not facts," and I would "shut up and listen." It seemed the old-timers and my sponsor had the answers to everything. And since I had no answers, who was I to balk at their crazy talk?

I knew one thing applied to me for sure: Step one: "We admitted we were powerless over alcohol—that our lives had become unmanageable."

I also knew that if these program guys were wrong, I would never trust anyone ever again in my life.

And if they were wrong, I would be dead.

I hung on desperately. I didn't pray, but I begged in my head for them to be right, for this to be right.

* * * * *

Once I graduated from rehab, Ronald said, "You're not going home to sleep in your own bed; you are going to a meeting."

And that's where I went.

And that's where I stayed: 450 meetings in the first 365 days of my sobriety.

I read every bit of literature I could put my hands on. Then I read some things mentioned in the literature, such as *The Varieties of Religious Experiences* by William James.

I became an extreme newcomer.

I attended every conference.

I went to 12-step retreats.

I joined all the study groups where we would take apart and meditate on the text that was teaching us about our condition. It was incredibly relatable, reading that book written so many years ago—astonishing, really, how relatable. But that's what worked about 12-step programs. Many of the truths about our compulsions and feelings were common.

I continued reading. I started reading books outside of the conference-approved literature because I was running out of material.

During meetings, I sat, shut up, and listened.

"We're going to keep you close to the bottom," Ronald would say, and I was okay with that.

The 12-step meetings provided the very-much-needed structure in my structure-less life. I was getting reset.

Perception

The definition of perception is three things: "The way you think about or understand someone or something; the ability to understand or notice something easily; the way that you notice or understand something using one of your senses." Was I doomed? Perhaps. Because how could I ever have the right perception of the guy I was if, at the age of 44, after the seizure, I learned I was somebody else entirely?

The facts: I had been abandoned. My biological mother died of alcoholism. I drank constantly.

There was no coming out of darkness without facing it—all of it—properly. But you can't face anything when you can't think or understand, or even use your senses. When your perception is a deformity.

I don't just mean this metaphorically, since as an adoptee and an alcoholic, I came by my newness honestly. I led the kind of split existence that can only be dealt with by ignoring it, numbing what I knew, and didn't know. I was a relinquishee, rejected by my birth parents, having to adapt to the reality of my adopted family. Because of that, I've always had problems with attachment and reaching out to people. My sense of rejection shadowed my whole life. So I drank over that, too. Alcohol silenced the war that was going on in my head. Me against myself. The adoptee versus the adopted.

In recovery, I adapted too, again—this time to being sober. Sometimes when people complain about 12-step programs "brainwashing" its members, an old-timer might peep, "But our brains needed washing!"

My brain needed washing. In the beginning.

I would reclaim myself later, but the first few months, even years, I couldn't possibly have tried harder to conform.

* * * * *

After six months of meetings, Ronald suggested I do Step 12, where I would start talking to newcomers about their recovery, take them through the steps the same way I had been taken through them. It seemed ludicrous to be given such responsibility so soon into my sobriety, but Ronald insisted and I did everything he said.

I understood that it was simply another process in my stabilization. I was walled in recovery. All 12-step meetings all the time.

At home, we hosted Christmas dinner—my first sober Christmas—and afterward, I ran to my meeting. I had to.

I sold my beautiful wine collection and dozens upon dozens of wine and cocktail glasses of different, expensive, and rare varieties. All of that had been purchased at some point during my drinking under that old pretext that I was the kind of guy who liked to entertain big, who liked to impress people with a beautiful wineglass and/or the perfect highball glass. That guy belonged to the Parallel Universe I was no longer part of. That guy was the guy I was killing with every meeting I went to. The smaller he got, the bigger I got. The weaker he got, the stronger I got.

I would never be entirely rid of him. I will be an alcoholic in recovery for life. But I was learning how to control him, how not to let his reality seep into mine. I was no longer a dreamer, but I dreamed. I dreamed of having a good life and of being useful. There was no place for the alcoholic me in this dream life.

Despite my devotion to sobriety, there were nights when I had a hard time falling asleep, torturing myself with thoughts such as, *"How am I going to sustain this lifestyle that I worked so hard to achieve and not drink? How am I to live in general?"*

Because alcohol was my answer to everything, and, despite immersing myself in recovery, I couldn't escape it.

I reminded myself: *You escaped it.* Literally. I sold my house on the lake to change my former lifestyle, full of drinking buddies, well-meaning neighbors who greeted me from rehab with a welcome basket, a bottle of Jack Daniels perched on top. There would be no more buddies puttering on their motorboats, shouting to me sitting sober and clear-headed on my deck: "Come on, David, come with us! What's wrong with you?"

There's nothing wrong with me. I just can't do this anymore. I would stand up and wave as friendly as I could.

After we sold our house, I no longer had to worry about coming out to my deck. We kept my wife's family house to be able to go and enjoy the lake on weekends, but my old life was done.

I lived happily ever after.

* * * * *

No, I didn't. There was still Shame to deal with. And then there was one more thing: Higher Power, the thing that was supposedly responsible for my sobriety. I started looking for it from the get-go because I didn't feel it. And I knew I had to find it or I'd be in big trouble.

As for my Shame, it came back with a vengeance a few years into my recovery.

Changes

I was skiing at Steamboat, Colorado, for the first time in ten years. Nine years into sobriety. I hadn't visited this place since my "après skiing" days, skiing only so that I could drink at bars at the base of the mountain. It used to be the most important part of my day.

At one point, I was skiing alone and I had a sense of great peace and oneness with nature. The vast brilliant whiteness ahead of me, the sun hitting the snow, making it shine like glass. The blue, sharp sky. The air filling my lungs, expanding them as I adjusted to the cold temperature. I started to ski downhill.

It was the same way it was on sailboats sometimes—a rush of adrenaline as I sped on, feeling exhilaration. Danger, too, but in my clear mind, I no longer had any urges to challenge this danger, to make risky turns just so that I could scare myself a little more. I no longer wanted to do that. Instead I liked feeling my body move, my muscles straining to maneuver to stay on course. I knew the limits of my body, too, now and I would not push past them.

A decade earlier, I had skied on the same mountain as I became increasingly tired and weak, then eventually fainted. My wife and I rested at the top of the gondola. The night before, I had finished a fifth of Scotch in addition to beers and wine throughout our trip.

"I just over-exerted myself at this altitude," I wheezed to Vicki.

We rode the gondola down the mountain instead of skiing down. We went back to our condo to rest, but I felt extraordinarily anxious.

By the time we arrived at a walk-in clinic, I was short of breath and gasping for air.

The clinic immediately put me in an ambulance and transported me to the hospital emergency room. I was admitted, hooked up to a heart monitor, and had the attending physician examine me. They instantly gave me oxygen, and continued to monitor my vitals and symptoms, yet could not diagnose the cause of my dizziness and shortness of breath. After a few hours observing me, they discharged me, advising me to rest overnight and come back the next day for a heart stress test.

I rested that night, and came back the next day to pass the test swimmingly. No issues. They attributed my fatigue to an adverse reaction to the altitude.

Ten years later, I schussed down the same hill feeling like I could breathe in the entire world. My heart pumped happily, a little reliable machine inside my chest.

The altitude was not a problem. In fact, I reveled in being so high up.

Regrets

There are so many more things to sobriety other than just putting alcohol away. It's a total revolt. The whole process feels like coming out of a blackout, one that lasted years instead of one night.

The more sober I got, the more my drunken, old, Parallel Universe seemed like a far-away nightmare. I was getting reincarnated despite not technically dying.

No death, but there was grief inside me that would overwhelm me. Something did die. The old me, but also the delusion. Not that I missed it but now, without it, I had to face the reality.

There was so much regret. All those years where I was present physically and where I pretended to be there emotionally when I wasn't actually able to feel. I would never get those years back. My children, of course, became the source of the biggest regret. I had missed their formative years, milestones that yes, I remembered, but that I knew didn't involve me even though my body might've been there. The other me was there, putting on a show, but the David who could truly appreciate what was happening didn't surface until it was too late.

I don't mean it was too late to get my life back. I mean that it was too late, impossible to relive the past:

my daughter losing her first tooth, my son learning how to ride a bicycle. I was there to witness it. Yet I witnessed very little. My mind was elsewhere.

Who was the old David? The guy riding the gondola down the mountain. The guy who almost got a plane diverted. The guy who existed in the basement instead of living with his family on the surface.

Was I him? No, I was no longer him. But remembering those things brought more Shame and more heartache. It was painful to think about those days in early sobriety. I didn't possess the kindness and forgiveness you have for yourself once you grow as a sober human being. In the beginning, I was in a survival mode.

* * * * *

I asked people about the old David. I wanted honesty. I couldn't rely on myself, on my memories, and I had an inkling that the Shame I felt was too grandiose even in comparison to how angry my loved ones were about me.

"I've always felt judged by you," my son said.

It hurt to hear him say that. But I got why he said it. That was my own world view, how I felt people responded to me. And I was doing it to my son unwittingly.

In sobriety, we were having our first honest conversations. He probably tried to have those kinds of conversations with me before, only now both of us were present for the pain and eventually relief that our new connection would bring both of us.

"I hated you. And you're not supposed to hate your father," my son said. "I didn't want to hate you."

I understood. I was proud of him, of his courage. The sadness washed over me as I hugged him and held him close. *I will never lose you again,* I thought. *I will never make you feel judged. I will try my hardest.* I was ashamed, but this time I knew at least where the Shame came from and I knew that there were things I could do to minimize this Shame.

I wasn't voicing any of this. I was done making promises, saying platitudes to those around me. I just thought things I wanted to say. I thought, *I'm here for you. Ultimately I'm here for you. Engage me or don't engage me. Whatever you need to do.*

By nature I was impatient, but this was part of the process—waiting for them to come to me, not trying to force the way we were going to heal.

I knew that the only way to right what I had done wrong was to be present, live well, and love my family. Telling them things and voicing my opinion. All of that was empty. At least for now. I had to rebuild my integrity. I had to build my identity.

With my wife I was finally able to articulate how I thought my drinking affected her. I asked her what kinds of restitutions she wanted. It was tricky to say things like that to her. We'd been married for more than two decades at that point, but it was the first time ever I was naming the emotions I was feeling, when I was able to say what I've never told anybody. I didn't say everything—there was no room for negativity, no self-pitying or desperation. All of that was for the rooms of 12-step meetings or therapy. Vicki only needed to know that I was sorry and that I was scared but happy, and she needed to see how I was going to improve. She had to witness my words in action.

"Restitutions?" She said. She smiled at me and there was such kindness in her, I've felt an overwhelming anguish—because I've hurt her—and joy—because I was a fortunate man to have a woman like her look at me with kindness.

She said, "I want you to be happy. I want you to do what's good for you. I want you to focus on your family."

The immediate family was easy because they got it. They knew why I was doing this. For them it was a matter of life and death, too. They would no longer feel unsafe. I was not a violent guy, but I was an unreliable guy. That is not a guy you want for a father, for a husband. I was no longer going to be him.

To the rest of the family, the revelation of my alcoholism was threatening. People didn't understand. Did it mean that I used to be physically abusive to my wife? Was I breaking things? How was it?

* * * * *

There are a lot of stereotypes about alcoholics and, sadly, many of them are true. Alcoholics can be violent, mean, dangerous. They can pack a whole family in a car and drive from a drunken barbecue. They can ask their pre-teen son to drive half way home because they're too drunk to continue.

We didn't talk about my alcoholism. My adoptive mother would sometimes ask, "What are you teaching these people in recovery?" As if I was there not because I belonged but because I was just helping others. Perhaps it was just easier for her to accept that, than the fact that I was one of those drunks, too.

Luck and Strength

You don't know how strong you are until you have your strength tested.

Sobriety gives you back your life. Not everyone is as lucky as I was. For many, sobriety means waking up in a vast, blackened swath of burnt-down forest. Nothing left. Not one green leaf. Families gone, friends gone, money gone, every single thing gone. But rooms of recovery are full of stories of people becoming sober under those kinds of circumstances and how despite all, they've managed to stay sober. They rebuild. They rebuild friendships or make new friendships. They rebuild families or start new families. They rebuild houses and careers. A homeless drunk guy sleeping on a bench is a CEO ten years later.

A newly sober alcoholic is weak. Or he seems weak to himself, but when he looks back many sober years later, he might see that it takes an enormous deal of strength to face the wreckage that addiction has left in his life. Feelings come up. Anger, sorrow, broken hearts all over the place. Everything has to be repaired and not everything can be. You can't repair dead friends or permanently damaged family who has cut you off. You can't repair people killed in a drunk-driving accident.

But what you can do is live sober and realize that life is short and there's no more time left to waste it. Live it. I live it.

* * * * *

I was waking up sober now. All the time. First time since childhood. First time without a hangover and body beat up from whatever I had been doing until two in the morning the night before. A drunken sleep is no sleep. A drunken sleep is just passing out.

There's a phenomenon called the "rebound effect," which is when the body tries to adjust to alcohol during the first half of the sleep period. Alcohol suppresses REM. Unfortunately, once alcohol is eliminated from the body (over a relatively short period), the body gets ripped out of the deep sleep and up you are, bright and early, the daylight like laser beams shooting at your hungover eyes. You are sleep-deprived.

Now, my body was rested. That was the first noticeable physical change. There was no stomachache, no headache, which I was so used to. What things to be used to!

Sober, I became years younger with energy coursing through me. It was as if I had a new, younger body. Colors became sharper. My appetite was back and my nose was no longer getting forced to try to smell my own, fermented breath. My nose smelled flowers now and the moist freshness of the lake and the leaves on trees.

For the first time in a long time, I was really seeing nature. It was intense, beautiful—so much beauty that

I drank it all in in large gulps. I was drunk on nature. Except I shouldn't say "drunk," because there was no euphoria to it, but rather there was peace so deep that for this non-believer, it became a source of spirituality. I was coming out of a fog.

I had a new fascination, a new curiosity that I've never had. *Look at that moon. Why is it orange tonight?*

* * * * *

But sobriety didn't exactly afford me calm—not at first. I was able to experience it indeed, here and there, but there was nothing calm about my newly sober mind.

I was bombarding myself with questions and dilemmas and I was berating myself, too. And weaving in and out of that, constantly, there were recovery teachings— hundreds of adages from my sponsor that echoed inside my head as absolute truths:

"Stinking thinking."

"Don't worry about any of this stuff now."

"Your thinking got you drinking…"

I was supposed to apply these to my life, and I could see the benefits of not thinking and of not worrying.

But I could not *not* think. It was impossible.

Within seconds on awakening, my mind would start spinning. The diseased, demonic voice of my brain was now an enthusiastic, albeit panicked, cheerleader: *Here are all the things I have to do. Here are all the things I have to accomplish. How am I going to do this? How am I going to get through this? I've wasted so much time. Life is short. Do something. Get up, get up, get up.*

And I would get up.

I could no longer numb my unquiet mind with alcohol. I could no longer deflect. I was no longer in my old delusion that everything was fine. That I had some control over my life. I didn't. I was powerless.

Strangely, being powerless was liberating. I couldn't do anything about things that were unchangeable. An active alcoholic is so full of shit that he will believe he can change the weather. A sober alcoholic knows that it's raining and he brings an umbrella along.

Lost and Found

I was struggling with my overactive mind and with guilt and Shame. I was trying to get in touch with my emotions—really feel things, whether they were negative or positive. I could no longer run away. But the more days I got, then months, and eventually, years, the closer I was to becoming the David that I am now. It was all worth it.

I surrounded myself with mantras, slogans, and texts approved by 12-step programs. I clenched my fists.

In the beginning, I isolated. My perceived deficiencies were magnified, along with my senses. Social situations were extremely anxiety-producing.

Soberly, I got to look at people and I had to wonder all the time what their motivation was. Before I could just have a drink with them and an instant, fake connection would be established. Now everybody had a potential to be a foe.

Give. Me. Some. Space. People.

I was afraid. I was under the world's microscope again. I didn't understand why I was that way. But I drank my entire life to facilitate relationships. Now I had to work for them.

Sometimes, in meetings, I would share and catch myself getting too excited, my arms waving, my voice thundering. *Uh oh. Did I go too far?*

There's a saying in recovery that some people drink because they felt as if they had no skin on, only nerves, exposed to the world, reacting to everything. A drink would provide coating for those nerves.

With my nerves exposed, it was good to feel everything again, but I became self-conscious of how I affected people around me. I didn't want to alienate anyone. I was terrified of doing this wrong. What exactly? My sobriety.

If I didn't do it right, I would relapse.

* * * * *

With time, I started unclenching my fists. There was a new ability I discovered in myself. I was able to sit in everything, without feeling that I had to do anything about it. I was able to be in a room full of people and just listen and not do anything.

I knew and believed this: if the world were to crash around me, I would lean back in my chair and rest my hands on my knees.

Is there anything that you have to do right now?

Me?

Yeah, you. You feel uncomfortable? You want to protect yourself?

No!

And I would sit and wait. There was nothing I could do about any of it. And there was freedom in that. The sort of freedom that I thought was prison before when, in my delusion, I thought I could control the universe.

Moving On

In the beginning, the only safe identity to assume and embody was that I was an alcoholic. I was told to alter everything about my lifestyle and even my thinking, because "my best thinking got me into this position." I needed to "avoid slippery places and slippery people" and to come out and tell everyone I'm an alcoholic so they wouldn't somehow tempt or corrupt me.

I was told I was powerless and that I should concern myself only with safety and security from drinking, and drinking people, places, and situations. I should always have my guard up. Nothing was safe other than the rooms of 12-step programs and talking to other recovering alcoholics. My previous identity, according to this new narrative, was that of a drinker: a sailboat racing drinker, a skiing drinker, a sports fan drinker, a snowmobiling drinker, an entrepreneur drinker, a trader drinker, a drinker husband, a drinker father, and so on.

* * * * *

There's a saying: "12-step work is not a way *of* life; it's a way *to* life." It is easy to confuse the two. For me, 12-step work was a way of life for the first five years of my recovery. There was no other way. I knew that at the five-year mark, I could somewhat confidently consider myself "recovering."

At a five-year mark, alcoholism is considered to be in remission, and a person is statistically as safe from relapse as he'll ever be. Not "recovered"—there's no such thing. I don't believe I could ever recover from this condition that I have. A benign tumor can be removed with no prognosis of recurrence; a benign alcoholism— sobriety—carries risk of developing into cancer, always.

Sounds grim, but it has to be grim because it's a reminder. The moment you think yourself cured is the moment you will relapse.

* * * * *

Milestones in sobriety can be compared to early human development, but you're both the child and the parent. Conversely, in the beginning I was an infant, helpless and in a survival mode. But as a parent to myself, I was defensive, cautious, deliberate, always prepared, risk-averse, and inflexible. I had to protect the infant-me and I would do so with all my might. If we slipped, we might never get up. I was ashamed of how infantile I was and of the fact that I was *just* an alcoholic. As my sobriety grew, so did my Shame about being an alcoholic. But for now, I tried to keep it in check. I shut up and listened, always shut up and listened.

* * * * *

As a 45-year-old, I became more conscious. I understood my world a lot better; *my* Reality was that I *was* an alcoholic. I couldn't drink and I was never going to fully recover, but that didn't mean that I wouldn't live a long, happy life.

Then, one day, it occurred to me I was no longer just that—an alcoholic. No matter what anyone tried to tell me, I knew there was more to it all. Of course, I knew that I was an intelligent person, not a cannibalistic piranha. Like a five-year-old, I was full of curiosity about life. My curiosity was much bigger than that of an infant. At that point I had completed my Masters in Addiction—I had great plans for a new career. I was itching to be someone else other than just an alcoholic. I was starting to see that my way *of* life was beginning to get in the way *to* life. I had to come back to my family fully. I had to take risks, seize opportunities. I wanted to be creative.

I wanted to do something I would love. I loved working on the trading floor, but that was my old life. I didn't miss it, but I missed the passion I had for a job. I wanted to get that back. I wanted to get my old life back, *sans* drinking. No, it wouldn't be my old life. It would be a completely different life. It would be the life I could fall in love with.

My Reality

From the movie *Forest Gump:*
"Lieutenant Dan: *'Gump, have you found Jesus?'*
Forrest Gump: *'I didn't know I was supposed to be looking for him, sir.'* "

I was like Forrest Gump.

In the beginning, I listened to everyone in recovery who told me how to be. I never got into arguments. I absorbed everything and I did the 12 steps as soon as I could. Later in sobriety, I started to doubt some of the program's ideas and teachings. It wasn't intentional; it just happened once my identity as only an "alcoholic" evolved, went beyond the box I had stuffed myself inside. And once that happened, I acknowledged my doubts, beginning with Step 2: "Came to believe that a Power greater than ourselves could restore us to sanity."

I didn't want to have those doubts. Yes, they were always there under the surface. I had grown up in an atheistic family after all, so doubting God was ingrained in me. Now, though, there was an urgency to quash these suspicions or confirm them once for all. From what I read in the literature and from what I heard from my fellow 12-step members, this Power—commonly referred to as Higher Power—was God. Sure, there were people who said a Higher Power could be your home group or even the program itself (or your dead grandfather, your cat or a toaster, as the jokes had it), but I could sense that what they were all talking about was a specific, correct kind of Higher Power, one who eluded me.

"Remember that we deal with alcohol—cunning, baffling, powerful! Without help, it is too much for us. But there is One who has all power—that One is God. May you find Him now!" it says in the "How it Works," chapter five of *The Big Book of Alcoholics Anonymous* (written by the first 99 male and one female members of Alcoholics Anonymous, where the whole program is outlined).

So. There is *One* who has all power. One. If there's only One, there are no others. The idea that anything could be your Higher Power—the group, the program— might seem contradictory. It did to me.

But I tried to fit in, as always. If asked, in my first years of sobriety, I would say that my Higher Power was female. It couldn't be a he. I relate to women more than to men—I like how soft-spoken they are, how intuitive and open with their feelings they can be.

But ultimately, I didn't believe in God—capital "G." I didn't believe in a goddess either.

The 12 steps are guiding principles of sobriety. Sometimes they are referred to as "spiritual principles," like rungs on a ladder bringing you closer to God, too, I suppose. With each step, members of a 12-step program have to do something that will help them overcome their addiction. Write down all the bad things they have done, confess them to a sponsor, write down people they have hurt, make restitutions, pray and meditate, and spread the message to another alcoholic who's still struggling with addiction.

The "How it Works" is an intro preceding the actual steps—it informs your attitude before doing the steps. First, full recovery can only be achieved through a rigorous following of the path of other sober alcoholics in the program. People who do not get sober are the ones who are unwilling to adhere fully to program principles, who are not able to be honest with themselves. They are referred to as "unfortunates" who were just born like that, the text says. (Are atheists such "unfortunates"? Are relinquishees?)

The text goes on to say that people with mental and emotional disorders stand *some* chance of recovery, but only if they're capable of honesty.

What does that mean? I suppose recovery is only possible for those with the right ingredients of the genetic lottery. Those who suffer from things like bipolar disorder, where occasionally they can't tell reality from delusions, are doomed by this logic. Continuing, people who stubbornly refuse to let go of some of their old ideas (such as the ones that there is no God) will see no results from the program until they cave in.

The most important thing is to give up any resistance whatsoever and understand that the only entity that has the power to get us sober is God. That *One* God.

The text ends with telling alcoholics to ask for God to protect them and care for them. This sort of asking has to be done with complete abandon, otherwise it's no good.

Sounds relatively easy, doesn't it? Don't drink, don't be an atheist, don't be too mentally ill, do what the rock stars of the program are doing, and try not to think too much.

During my first formative five years, I needed these sorts of extreme teachings to survive. But the longer I was in the rooms of 12-step meetings, the less I got it. And I felt Shame over that. I hated myself again. This time for not getting it. There was something wrong with me again, just as there was, always, everywhere else. Even here, in the place that seemed like the safest place on Earth for someone like me, I was suddenly in great emotional pain.

I was a fraud again. I was acutely aware of being a fraud. I was pretending to *get* it. I had to, otherwise, according to the program precepts, I would fail. I would drink. I would die.

Ironically, in the place where honesty was one of the biggest requirements to recovery, I was being completely dishonest, not only to my fellows in recovery but, most importantly, to myself. My Shame was like a vise (vice?) closing around my neck; it was becoming harder and harder to breathe in all those church basements where the meetings were held. Where God eluded me.

God

G od kept not showing up. I prayed for her to show up, every morning, in the shower.

I looked for her, it, *One*...for God, everywhere as the Shame of not being able to find her, of not fitting in, again kept growing.

I read about God.

I talked about God with rabbis and pastors, and during work lunches, I sat in beautiful St. Andrew's church near my workplace, waiting for God to appear. I prayed day and night...but to what?

I suppose I was praying to lure God out, make God appear like a genie from a bottle. And speaking of bottles, my fear was that I was going to go back to it, the bottle, if I didn't find this God.

Some days it felt as if I was losing my mind. I was delusional. I was waiting for a tooth fairy; I was waiting for Santa. And occasionally, I could almost convince myself of a vision of a celestial being descending from the church's ceiling, wrapping her wings, or her halo — or whatever the god trends were back then — around me. But nothing. Nada.

Sit back. Relax. God will get in touch with you. God exists. After all, God graced you with sobriety. The tempting voice in my brain had metamorphosed into the voice of all those 12-step members who got God. They were constantly talking to me in my head. Calling me out on my bullshit.

It made no sense to me. I was getting hopeless. My sober perception was getting blurred.

* * * * *

One phenomenon of sobriety is drinking dreams. They are terrifying and vivid. They can be so vivid that sometimes you can't differentiate reality from fiction once you wake up. I had one the other day. The dream was about me getting plastered and trying to hide it. I was being tormented by my deception and felt completely devastated by my relapse. On awakening, my mind immediately snapped to: *See? There is something wrong with you!*

I looked down to see if I was indeed holding a bottle of Jack Daniels. I looked around to see if my wife was watching me, knowing that I was drinking.

I was in bed, no empty bottles near me; my wife was still asleep.

I took a deep breath.

I knew it was just a dream. Reality was me in bed with my wife. But it took one silly dream to shake me up and show me how perception depends on a precarious balance of illusions and reality.

That God I was looking for was like a drinking dream. A false conviction that something happened, which didn't happen.

* * * * *

In sobriety, I often thought, *Am I doomed?* I couldn't live with alcohol, I couldn't find God, I had lived for four and a half decades without finding out who my mother was. How did someone like me have any ability to understand the environment around him? Which clues were the right clues? Which slogans pertained to me, especially since I truly couldn't apply the ones that insisted I, for example, "Let go and let God"?

A disease of perception is the inability to interpret the environment: people's motives, how people respond to me, what the world is like. Everyone can, potentially, be an enemy; everyone possibly, secretly hates me. And for the longest time, my perception told me that I was so unique, such an outsider, that I couldn't possibly relate to anyone.

At the same time, people in recovery are frequently told they're not unique. It's very confusing to find yourself between two different versions of who you are: a person who is unique and a person who needs to fit in to get the program. My inability to find God was making me unique. Another conflict with sobriety as dictated by 12-step programs.

* * * * *

During all of that, I briefly saw a psychologist, because I still had a lot of trouble reconciling my recovery with reality. We talked about God, too.

One day, my therapist said: "What if you're not meant to find God?"

What if I'm not meant to find God?! What a concept. That's great, but now what? Because recovery programs say I'm going to relapse. If she tells me I'm not meant to feel that way, how should I feel?

"I want to feel connected to something," I said to the therapist. "I want to know that I'm watched over and cared for. That's what 12-step programs tell me; they tell me to trust the power of the people who came before you."

The therapist listened. She asked questions but didn't push for answers. I had none. I only had fear and Shame at that point, even though what she said seemed to loosen a knot inside me.

I knew if I left the 12-step community, I would drink. I didn't want to abandon what I thought was working for people. If I abandoned it, I would be abandoned again.

False Consensus Effect

There's a concept in psychology known as the "False Consensus Effect," where you believe other people think and feel what you think and feel.

With that False Consensus Effect comes a False Uniqueness: a belief that I have better values and am generally more honest, capable, and kind than others. This further magnifies something in 12-step programs referred to as "Terminal Uniqueness": seeing myself as so special that nobody could possibly understand me.

That was a false perception I fought—and still do—that told me that the situations I face are unlike anything faced by other alcoholics ever before. The problem with all of this is that it isn't easily discernible for someone like me: a relinquishee, an introvert, someone who feels like a dilettante in life, a ginger, an overly sensitive person (and, today, an agnostic whose Higher Power is not God, but *Reality*—I capitalize it because it's specific to me, just like god is God to those who believe).

But I was and am unique.

Yet, I could exaggerate my uniqueness to the point of deformity. A ginger, an adoptee, an alcoholic, someone who's highly sensitive yields about 2,032 like me in the country. (Trust me, I did the calculations). If I add to this being married, introverted, a male, a sailor and so on, I will eventually arrive at a number that will equal fewer than one person! (Trust me, I did the calculations.)

I could drive myself crazy with my uniqueness. So perhaps it was in my best interest to shut up and listen. Just give up and try to fit in even if I had to amputate my head that kept insisting there was no God. A square peg in a round hole.

That seemed like a drastic solution. There was, of course, another way to lose my head and that was to drink.

I hated being dishonest. But being an agnostic in traditional recovery that required me to believe, I was being dishonest.

I was also feeling so much discomfort with many tenets of 12-step recovery, for example, where we were being asked to work on our defects of character. Depressive disposition was a defect of character: From the *Big Book*, "As *we morbidly pursue* this *melancholy* activity, *we* may sink to such a point of *despair* that nothing but *oblivion* looks possible as a solution. Here, of course, *we* have *lost all perspective*."

Questioning of the program itself was a character defect, a sign of pride and lack of humility. In fact, the idea of the Christian seven deadly sins seemed to have been accepted as a guide of personal inventory of defects: pride, greed, lust, anger, gluttony, envy, and sloth.

The *Big Book* says, "It is not by accident that pride heads the procession."

I was too proud. I was not humble. My always wanting more and better was the purest form of gluttony. I realized my sins.

But God would still not show up.

I was losing my identity, the one that had just begun to expand. I was in danger of having it disappear completely. My perception was warped in more spectacular ways than ever before.

* * * * *

As it was with my last drink, I suddenly came to, finally.

I simply said, *Screw it. I have to find something else, not her, not God, not One. I need to find people who will find me. I need to find Reality.*

I loved 12-step work, but I kept getting re-traumatized. My ego was headless, trying to fit its defiant misshape into that conformist hole.

Seven years of looking for something that isn't there was a long time. To me, seven years of not finding God was enough proof that God didn't exist. Or if it did, God didn't want to be known. What kind of God is going to make me suffer like that? This God must not be there. And if God is there, God has abandoned me completely and I've had enough of that in my life.

Either way, I no longer cared.

I cared about my sobriety. I cared about my family. I cared about my job. I cared about being happy and fulfilled. I had so much more to discover yet. This much I could control, if nothing else. Unbeknownst to myself, I was on my way to finding something that would replace God, a Higher Power that would finally make sense to me.

But first—and this was also the first step to finding my Higher Power—I had to find out more about the box I had put away, the box with the information about my mother. There was more to me than I knew. My Reality was that I was an alcoholic who didn't quite fit in 12-step programs, but my Reality was also that I was a man who didn't quite fit in the world because of his murky past. The difference now, seven years into sobriety, was that I knew why I felt like I didn't fit in. I would have to find a way to make it work within 12-step meetings. I knew that now. And I would have to find a way to make it work within my Reality.

The New World

"Goodbye," said the fox. "And now here's my secret, a very simple secret. It is only with the heart that one can see rightly; what is essential is invisible to the eye."

"What is essential is invisible to the eye," the Little Prince repeated, so that he would be sure to remember.

— From *The Little Prince* by Antoine de Saint-Exupéry

They weren't partisans, but to me it seemed as if they were. When I found them, for a while, I would look over my shoulder, feeling as if I was cheating on my recovery in mainstream recovery. Except I knew deep down inside that I wasn't doing anything wrong.

I understood that they were my people. I was looking for them all along and I've found them. They were online mostly, at first, and then I discovered one meeting in Chicago where I could see them in person.

In my many years in the rooms of 12-step programs, I've never experienced what is referred to as "pink cloud," a type of joy, a new-found appreciation for life that the newly sober person experiences after getting sober for the first time.

It's true that on getting sober, I felt as if I were a new-born and colors, tastes, smells were sharper. It's true that I could stop and lose myself in the awe of nature. But I've never had the sort of euphoria I've heard others talk about all the time. Or more specifically, I've never experienced that euphoria in the actual meetings.

I went to meetings all the time and I certainly felt some form of kinship, but even in the beginning, my membership was tainted with Shame and my joy seemed inauthentic. Sometimes it was forced. I wanted to be sober desperately and I was sober. But no matter how hard you try, you can't think yourself into total happiness. Happiness happens organically; it is independent of your efforts. I remember going into regular 12-step meetings and hearing people laugh at some of the tragic stories they would share. It seemed grotesque to me that they would find tragic things happy: lost families and businesses, lost lives.

Stop laughing. You're all deluded. Stop it.

Later, I understood that those were war stories, that besides the actual program, humor was a defense against despair that a sober person was to feel once he realized the gravity of the damage he had left behind. In any case, the camaraderie of that dark-humor laughter eluded me for a long time.

Except when I got to the agnostic meeting. There I laughed. It was bizarre. But I truly felt like laughing.

I heard the preamble read, the *Big Book* text that talks about belonging to a fellowship of people who share their experience, strength, and hope, with the purpose of helping other, still struggling alcoholics to get sober. The preamble states that: "The only require-ment for membership is a desire to stop drinking." It talks about the group not being a part of any organized entity. There's not a mention of God in the preamble. It is different from the "How It Works" text, in which it is implied that proper recovery depends on the strength of one's faith. "How It Works" was not read in the agnostic meeting.

* * * * *

The 25 or so people in the room were exactly like any other 25 sober alcoholics. In other words, slightly too excitable and varied, from many different walks of life. They asked me about me. They said: "What brought you here?"

No one said to shut up and listen.

No one asked me about God, have I found God, have I gone down on my knees and prayed?

So I laughed because I felt free to do so. Laughter comes from the place of freedom. Try laughing when you don't feel like it. I tried. I didn't feel like it. Now I felt like it.

I was on another planet. The one I belonged on. There were three Parallel Universes after all: the drinking one, the 12-step one, and now this one. My identity was shifting again, except this time it felt like it was shifting into the right place. I loved being so-ber. I loved being alive, really being alive. Now I was finding comfort in sobriety that I haven't felt…ever?

It was that feeling I've had a few times in my life—the feeling of being swaddled, of a mother holding a child, a feeling of being home. There was no God, but there were people like me and they were the ones who cared about me; they were the ones who would keep me sober the way God was supposed to. I believed that with my entire being. The comfort of kinship I so searched for—I had finally found it.

* * * * *

I didn't need to unlearn things. I didn't think I wasted my time in mainstream 12-step programs. In fact, it was the opposite. I absolutely needed it. I needed that kind of boot camp, the discipline. And I was among the people who understood the fundamental concept of addiction. The concept of wanting to alter our perception—via drink—to fit our delusion, which we called "reality." We all possessed the inability to deal with feelings and with people around us. We shared the numbing of those feelings of inferiority that the lack of connection brought on. The sense of loss that many of us couldn't quite identify—although for me, it became clear that it was my trauma over the adoption that made me feel so disconnected. We had fear of life instead of love of life. All those things were familiar to any alcoholic. Those were things that had nothing to do with God. At least not for me.

As different as we were—blue-collar, privileged, white, black, male, female—there was the same malady at our core. The malady of misperception. In the agnostic meetings, it was the same. But there was no pressure to fit. I just fit in.

* * * * *

I became a student of secular recovery. And again, I immersed myself in everything there was to learn about it. I read books. I found on-line forums. (At first, I didn't even know what to Google: "How to be an atheist in recovery?" "What to do if you don't believe?")

What? I had no idea. But eventually, I've found what I was looking for. There were so many others like me. All over the world. There were books.

Like the book by Marya Hornbacher, *Waiting: A Nonbeliever's Higher Power*, which with its gentle, non-pushy language provided the perfect bridge between what I knew about recovery in mainstream 12-step programs and what I was after in the agnostic one.

I was no longer teachable in the mainstream programs, but I was teachable all over again in the agnostic program and I loved it. I loved it because it felt right. I adapted, sure—I knew how to do that well— but it was the sort of adaptation that aligned with my universe completely.

* * * * *

The pretending stopped, too. The pain of that was too great.

I became conscious. Above all, I became the real sober alcoholic who could bring the message of recovery to those who needed it. And once everything fell into place in my recovery, I started to believe in something, I acquired a Higher Power. It wasn't God and it especially wasn't that One God from the text of the *Big Book*. My Higher Power was Reality. The Reality was many things: that I was an adoptee, that I had adoptive parents who loved me, that I had a family of my own that loved me, that I drank for many years, that I got sober, that I had to be authentic to myself and that there were others like me.

Getting It

I never imposed my non-mainstream views on others—what they believed or not was none of my business—but I was able to understand that traumas that brought people down needed to be healed, not scratched and made to bleed the way I had been taught in mainstream recovery.

Now, I really *got it*. I needed to understand myself to understand others and to be able to help them. I was an addictions counselor who could truly counsel. With kindness and compassion, I could listen because I felt listened to.

I thought of the mainstream 12-step programs a lot, the way they required the alcoholic to humble himself to the point of self-loss. Deflation at depth is a dangerous requirement to the already-deflated. I didn't want that for the people who were broken and lost already. They needed to be found. I wanted the same freedom for them that I've felt, and I was able to bring it because I now had it. God or no God, anybody could do it. As long as they weren't being shamed into sobriety. As long as they were real and understood reality for what it was: not a thing to bend or blur with alcohol or drugs, but a state that makes you present in every moment, that keeps you in check and hopefully that will keep you sober. Something that I chose to call my Higher Power. It demanded no self-flagellation; it didn't threaten me and tell me that I was guilty of things I had no control over.

Because if I were to believe the mainstream teachings, I'd have to confirm my delusions.

What was my part in being an abandoned baby? The mainstream programs told me I had a part in it, that there was indeed something wrong with me—this confirmed my sick suspicions—but I finally understood that sometimes things just happen. Sometimes you play no part. The parts are chosen for you and there's absolutely nothing you can do about it. You have the context of the trauma, you have the papers that show you were adopted, you are a confused child, melancholic and lost—but none of it is your fault.

* * * * *

And with these sorts of insights, I was, finally, integrated. I felt free.

With the new-found strength, I was finally able to do what scared me the most: I picked that box off my shelf and I faced it all. I walked right into my pain.

Pain

I need to clear my head.

I'm sitting here, staring at the lake. I'm taking deep breaths.

I'm protecting myself. I need this sanctuary.

The default is anger, frustration that I'm powerless, that other people have made decisions for me, that other people decided I was going to be a part of the social experiment of forcing unwed mothers to give up their children. Other people had not only my birth certificate, but my entire history. I had to fight for it, to be able to see it.

My wife's lineage can be traced back to the 1500s. Why was it so difficult for me to obtain a piece of paper showing when I was born, what I weighed as a newborn? A signature of some random social worker has sealed my fate for so many years.

Sometimes I'm full of rage when I think about these things. I hate being powerless. Why shouldn't I know? I am powerless over alcohol, sure, but to not be able to have power over my very own being, my life and history? That's an atrocious theft.

Now, in sobriety, the rage is short-lived. The search for my roots is me taking the power back. The search is my control. The search is me trusting the Higher Power of my Reality.

* * * * *

When I first petitioned the Milwaukee, Wisconsin, court and received the identifying information about my past, about my mother, was the beginning of taking control of my past. From the State of Wisconsin, from the social worker, and from my adoptive mother (who seemingly couldn't remember the details that were my origin and identity). I put the box on the shelf and drank on, but later, in sobriety, I knew that getting those records was what gave me back the control that had been relinquished by others on my behalf at birth.

And it's happening again. More control is coming back into my life. There's another box, except this time, I'm not putting it on any shelf. It's wide open and I'm looking inside, curious and eager to unpack all of its contents. I'm alone and I need to be in order to deal with the roller-coaster in my head.

What happened? Another shift in identity, another piece of the puzzle found. Earlier today, I talked to my half-brother on my father's side of the family, for the first time ever. I cannot comprehend it all yet. I'm angry, I'm in pain, I'm metaphorically bleeding onto this page. At the same time, I'm overwhelmed with joy. All of it, it's maddening.

I have an image of a Slingshot Ride in my head. That's a modern amusement park ride that uses cables and a patented spring propulsion device incorporating up to 720 specially designed springs. Slingshot passengers are propelled over 328 feet at speeds of about 100 miles per hour. You can watch videos on YouTube showing reactions of people strapped into the device: screaming, throwing up, laughing hysterically, even peeing on themselves. There's a whole collection of those videos. They are as funny as upsetting to watch.

I picture two people sitting in a Slingshot. One is screaming in panic, terrified and convinced he's going to die and the other is laughing like a maniac, absolutely ecstatic to be on the ride.

This is what's going on in my head as I sit and look at the calm lake, its familiarity comforting, but not comforting enough to stop the Slingshot from being catapulted over and over again inside me.

But I don't mind. Or it's not that I don't mind. I am confident that I will be able to deal with this chaos. I've been there before.

In my new phase of recovery, I no longer rely on false spiritual bypasses. I don't have the luxury of getting down on my knees and praying. I could, of course, but it would mean nothing. I envy the people who have faith, who have the anesthetic of God to carry them through trauma.

I don't have that.

I'm not feeling sorry for myself, by the way—that's just the way it is.

I have something that's precious, more than the God I was never able to find afforded me.

What I do have is experience. And strength and hope, too. The three tenets of any sober alcoholic's story. This is how many alcoholics in recovery map out the narratives of their journey from drinking to recovery. The phrase "sharing your experience, strength and hope" outlines the timeline of this journey.

Experience: how you drank, what brought you to the rooms of 12-step programs.

Strength: how you overcame drinking, what makes you stay in the rooms of 12-step programs.

Hope: how you live now, what the future holds.

I have all three solidly ingrained in me. My experience is my strength is my hope. Everything is connected.

* * * * *

My half-brother on my father's side seems like a gentleman. He's kind and forthcoming with information. We're only in the stage of tiptoeing around the events of my relinquishment and his finding out that I exist, so the information trickles in. It can't gush in; that would be too much for both of us.

I'm lucky that this kind of man is my half-brother, that he doesn't get hysterical or obnoxious. I've heard many horror stories from other adoptees, their blood relatives shutting doors in their faces, saying they wanted nothing to do with them.

My experience hasn't been that. Not with the relatives on my mother's side of the family—my sisters—and now, with this new family, the half-brother.

There's a new half-sister, too, and she's reached out as well, and she seems kind and composed. I am relieved that they are such nice people. I am overjoyed that I'm discovering more about my roots.

But I mentioned anger before. The anger comes from betrayal. Or neglect. Or whatever you'd like to call it. Callousness? I can't even tell at this point because I don't know *her* side of the story. My father's sister confirmed my existence. That's why my half-brother didn't question who I was; there was no need for a DNA test. But this woman had known for 56 years about me and she said nothing. My father hasn't been alive for more than two decades. He died of a brain tumor when I was in my thirties.

(My father dying somewhere, my mother dying, and my not knowing anything about it, going on about my life as if this profound and tragic thing wasn't happening. Nothing was happening. Yet, everything was happening.)

Was there never a time when she felt it would be appropriate to say something? What a secret to keep.

I won't stay angry for too long. I cannot rely on my default mechanisms—anger, indignation, sorrow—because they will lead me to drink. I have to work through all those issues eventually.

It's a never-ending process and I'm okay with that.

Right now, I'm just beginning on this new adventure, my half-brother's written words engraving themselves into my brain. I have learned three things about my father. In no chronological order but in the reverse order of significance:

1) My father was color-blind.
2) He died of a brain tumor.
3) He drank too much.

* * * * *

It's funny how I took that first box off the shelf and dealt with my mother's story, and I was convinced that that would be it. I faced that pain. I pictured her dying of a heart attack alone and broken in the shelter. I pictured the dirty blankets and receipts from the liquor store in the storage room where she slept. I pictured her being alive, being in this world. I learned of her tragic demise, her sad life. (Eventually I even got actual pictures of her, of her smile disappearing into a ghost grin, her face dissolving into alcoholism.)

I also imagined her as a happy, red-headed coed and a scared pregnant girl who knew she wouldn't be able to keep the baby. I even imagined her as a child—my own daughter is a beautiful, red-headed young woman, so I sometimes wondered if my mother was ever like that, and equally joyous and carefree. Before everything else that happened to her—her life as a flight attendant, a drinker, a bloated woman with too many ex-husbands and broken children. Before she gave up on "Baby Boy Bender."

I went over so many of such imaginings. And the whole time, I never thought my father would pop out of a (new) box; he was never officially confirmed as my father.

It is only now, emailing with my half-brother, that I learn it was true, that the handsome athlete who was charming and social and seduced a pretty red-headed coed, did exist for sure. He was confirmed. And with that, I am confirmed. Again.

* * * * *

I spent 16 months getting to know my biological mother through the documents, and later through the information some of my half-siblings provided. I was constantly processing what I was learning, but even today, it's still new, still traumatic. But I'm used to it now. Once I took that box off the shelf and faced what was in it, I had no choice but to follow through. I could no longer drink about my anger and sorrow because I was sober and sane. So I had to deal with it straight on.

* * * * *

In counseling, there's an insistence to see an adoptee client as a child. If I were to engage in such therapy, it would probably mean going over and over my trauma of believing I was unwanted, when I told my friends about being adopted, at the age of six. In a way, to me, this is similar to drinking over a trauma; an alcoholic is like a child and he can't manage to face his fears. I didn't want to be a child anywhere—in life, in therapy. I was a grownup and I wanted to deal with my history like a grownup.

* * * * *

Back at the lake, the Slingshot in my head slows down a little. The screams of the panicked guy are fainter and the laughing guy calms down, too.

I understand that I will have no choice but to embrace this new adventure ahead of me. My biological father, a new box. There's nothing I can do about the facts. I can only accept whatever information comes my way. I'm curious about my father. I want to know more details, but at this point I can't even tell what I'll be able to ask. So far, the half-brother has been nothing but a gentleman, but to be honest, I still feel like an intruder, showing up in those people's lives. But that is my life, too. I have a right to it. What a strange place to be, feeling like an intruder in your own life.

I'm not kind with myself about that yet. Initially, there was too much confusion over my father's sister keeping the secret. This immense burden was forever relived, however, when my presence was acknowledged. This previously undisclosed reality initially filled me with anger, accompanied by the familiar feelings of Shame and guilt. But I have come to understand that my father's sister carried an immense secret for most of her life, and can see with empathy how she was not consciously complicit in perpetuating this delusion.

But all of this is short-lived, and eventually, the Slingshot will come to a halt. I have hope that more will be discovered, but I have to be careful. I have to wait for the doors to open wider for me first. I have to stay still for now and maybe more will be revealed.

* * * * *

It was different with my biological mother. One of my sisters was looking for me as actively as I was looking for my mother. When we finally found each other, it blew my mind. She wanted me to be her big brother. And she needed a big brother; her life hasn't been the easiest. She told me about her life with *our* biological mother. It was July 2014 and it was overwhelming, the catharsis.

When our searches culminated in finally meeting, I bawled for days. I met her and I wasn't shunned; I wasn't getting relinquished by her. The opposite: I was getting embraced, adopted.

The society and the times dictated that I was supposed to be invisible, but here was a person who wanted me. She was my first blood relative outside of my children. Our biological makeup was similar. We had the same mother. *Our mother.* How extraordinary it was that I shared a mother with a stranger.

All those changes took some getting used to. But I loved the process of getting used to them. As terrifying as it was, these new relationships only expanded my world, made it that much more interesting. There were connections all over the place. I was now spending my life finding out that everything about me was a part of a huge network, that I've been unknowingly connected in hundreds of intricate ways. In my mind, I see one of those images that illustrates the String Theory of the Universe, a helix made out of twisting, oscillating spokes of multicolored light, emanating from a spiral core. At different times in my life, I oscillated between being connected to my adoptive family to being connected to my recovery family to being connected to my biological family. Reality is knowing that these relationships, including my relationship with Reality, will also oscillate over time. And having Reality in my life allows me peace.

It is the opposite of what my life used to be like, but today, having gotten so much closer to people, finally, I understand the pain of disconnect and I know now it's not going to kill me. It's the kind of pain that is no longer acute. A dull ache.

Now, my Reality is that I'm on an endless quest. I will never know the whole truth with my biological parents being dead, but I have all the supports. I have people in my life. I can go into the deepest darkness and come out alive.

At the age of six, I decided there was no one in the entire world I could talk to. Today, I can talk to the world. I'm talking to you.

There's Nothing Wrong With You

There's nothing wrong with you.
The beliefs you have about what is wrong with you
aren't true. They aren't real, and they do nothing to
make you grow as a human being.

I don't mean to be so abstract. I speak confidently
about what I'd learned after seven years of looking for
God in the rooms of 12-step meetings and not being able
to find her. Sometimes I think it took me too long to free
myself from the chains of rigid teachings, but perhaps I
needed those seven years to feel that I was right about
being in charge of my future.

It might seem arrogant to say I was right, but how
arrogant is it to tell people they won't get better if they
don't find God in their lives? When they genuinely
can't? That's truly dangerous.

So today, I believe in taking charge of my own life.
There's no greater happiness than knowing you have
some control of how your life unfolds. I don't claim in
any way to be able to control everything that happens
to me—that would be absurd—but I am able to take responsibility and not rely on magic to turn my life into
some kind of paradise.

In terms of addiction, successfully recovering people are not the ones who are sober; they are the ones who are sober and not afraid of facing pain. They deal with challenging situations because they understand that there's more to life than *The Big Book of Alcoholics Anonymous*. They don't follow, blindly, the instructions of their program. There's a lot of wisdom in the *Big Book*, but quoting from it like a parrot and trying—against reason—to reason will not get anyone happier.

You know those inspirational posters you sometimes see in people's offices, with some guy climbing rocks with words about perseverance or ambition? Or the cute quotes people like to post on social media? Those wonderful bits of wisdom perfectly framed that are ready to be popped into your mind like mental chocolates? That's exactly what they are: chocolates. They melt. And then there's nothing left, nothing learned. Even if you memorize a hundred of them, you will not in any way be wiser. It's dangerous to take complex thoughts and oversimplify them with a slogan or quote or quick-fix answer. They lose their power—the Reality of what life is really like.

Wisdom is an ongoing thing. You need to search for it every day, all the time. As with closure, you will never reach the end of learning—there's always more to know—but wisdom gives context the way no motivational poster, no cutesy quote, will give you. It is the search for wisdom, not a search on Google, that will make you better at life.

I'm not saying I'm better at life in general. I'm just better at my own life. There are still many times I feel completely lost. Just the other week, as I was talking with my half-brother, it was emotionally taxing; the Slingshot activating itself over and over in my head. I still don't know how to deal with all the new information about my past, exactly. I mean how to deal with it in the least harmful way—for me, and for my half-brother.

But what's different today from the way I was years ago is that I understand the world that much better. It is my Reality, my Higher Power, that helps me stay grounded even in the face of emotional ups and downs. I check in with myself every moment that might get me rattled, as I did when talking with my newly found half-brother: *What are you going to find out? What is the worst thing you will find out?*

I already know the worst: I was abandoned. I drank because I couldn't fit in.

I've outlived my father, and I have now lived longer than my mother.

These are the things I know, and there's nothing to do but just accept the facts for what they are.

Even when there's anger—my default mechanism— it's not a negative thing. It's just a thing to work through. Sometimes in contemplation, alone with myself, sometimes through talking with others. The traditional 12-step program told me I had to be tolerant, patient, and loving. How about instead of that, I simply acknowledge my anger and let it simmer until it passes? I've been here before, in this anger. How am I able to live in anger and its absolution? Parallel Universes. I know what both feel like. And I know that everything passes.

* * * * *

I no longer pray in the shower. There's no one, no thing to pray to. (And if there is she, One, God, whatever will find me. I just don't worry about it anymore.)

I'm not completely "cured" of my maladaptive patterns of thinking. My mind spins all the same, the way it used to back then. Some mornings, it's all a cascade of anxieties about the future, even though I aim to stay in the moment: *I have to talk to a politician, I have to talk to a room of 500 people, I have to help someone's parents understand their kid's addiction…*

There are always things to worry about. I worry about the fact that I am not competent. That I don't have enough expertise. That there are others out there who could do a much better job.

But today, as soon as those cascading thoughts enter my mind, they crash against a dam I've erected over the years. And that dam is experience. Looking into my past and seeing the evidence and the negative self-talk is overpowered by the positive: *David, get rid of the crap in the past that has told you you're not good enough. Look at all these other situations where you've succeeded; look at the evidence. Who gives a shit what the people think about you?*

So many people say you bring unique perspective into difficult situations. You've spoken in front of 500 people before despite being afraid to do so. You've tested yourself over and over and you've passed so many of these tests. You'll be fine.

That kind of thinking brings me into the moment. In the moment, I know I'm good enough. I'm not turning my will and mind over to God. I'm turning my will and my mind to what is. Right now. Reality. The past doesn't matter other than what it has taught me. The future is uncertain. All I have is this moment.

From *The Big Book of Alcoholics Anonymous:* "We sought through prayer and meditation to improve our conscious contact with God as we understood Him, praying only for knowledge of His will for us and the power to carry it out."

The conscious contact is not with God, for me. It is with Reality.

* * * * *

When I first got sober, I turned into a new human being. The Parallel Universes merged temporarily and I got some peace back in my life. But there's no such thing as true peace if you're not honest with yourself.

Of course, this is not all, saying you need to be honest with yourself. Sometimes being honest with yourself is too painful to bear. Honesty doesn't always equal freedom from obsession. But it's a start. And if you believe you have the power to change your life, your life might just change. It's an ongoing process; there's no exam at the end of it. I was always scared that I was a fraud—in meetings so acutely—and I never paid attention to the fact that recovery is an "inside job." It's funny, that is one of the terms used in the rooms, but I never got it until I got rid of this pointless quest for God. It was indeed an "inside job," and there was no doubt in my mind that I was finally on the right track.

If you are in a 12-step program meeting or thinking of getting there one day, remember that the people who guide you don't actually have instructions that are any better than yours. What they have is better than instructions; they have perspective. They should offer perspective, not instructions. Instructions are for fixing bicycles, not for fixing people.

Safety

Do you feel safe?
This is the number one question of my Reality. It should be everybody's. We spend our lives searching for feelings of comfort and love many of us had as children. Or we search for the comfort and love we've never had. But we search. For safety.

That's the biggest thing that can help to elevate you further in your recovery or whatever it is you might be struggling with. Safety, of course, is a luxury for many people, but it is the most essential thing to survival. It's not about fear. We all know fear; I've met fear face down in my keyboard, waking up and not knowing what happened the night before. The fear of coming to from a seizure. The fear about being constantly at war with myself.

Fear is part of life. Being scared to death is part of life. But getting things done will get me—and, hopefully, you—closer to safety. It is putting one foot in front of the other. It is one day at a time. Some of these are the slogans that hang in the rooms of 12-step programs. So many of them sound empty, stupid, even, so rigid in their messages of black and white—just like those inspirational posters. I used to look at them and scream in my head: *Don't tell me what to do.*

Other times, I'd feel inadequate, not because I wasn't getting the message, but because I couldn't stop the mind that insisted I think. Which used to be a troubling thing—specifically, the sort of thinking that was not aligned with every single message in the literature.

If I were to create a slogan, it would be about hope: "Don't hope for more than is possible." This is to say that ultimately you will get disappointed if you rely on the faulty magic of hope. Hope leads to fear of the future. Stop hoping to win the lottery and let go of the thought that you'll win. Maybe you'll win. Maybe not. Probably not. But you never know.

Just let go of it.

Small hopes are better. One hope at a time. Aspire, but don't get indignant if it doesn't happen. It might happen; it's just that it might not happen when you want it or how you want it. The control is not in controlling circumstances. The control is in knowing that you can't control them. And once you know that, then things are aligned with Reality. Not magic, not God, not inspirational, bite-sized quotes.

Life is more complex. If you set your mind free, your thinking will get you through complex ideas. Small talk, small thoughts—all of that is dangerous, easy like a shot of Jack Daniels. Small talk mimics the real connection; small thoughts mimic wisdom. Alcohol mimics feeling okay with all of those illusions, all of those lies that we tell ourselves to not have to deal with Reality.

The only way to understand how safe—or unsafe—you are is to know your own Higher Power. What gives you ultimate comfort? What sustains you?

Are you hanging too far out of a window, or are you sitting on a couch?

Are you in the trenches under a shower of bullets, or are you with a friend who will inevitably try to drag you into a bar?

Are you talking to your wife and she's listening and you know that you're the luckiest bastard on earth because she's listening?

And do you know that nobody can fix you? Not even her?

It's true.

You can only fix yourself. Once you're safe.

A Bridge

My half-sister called me and said, "I'm coming up on a year of not drinking and I thought of you, what you've accomplished."

I love hearing her voice. We talk often. The communication is intense and it feels that we need to make up for all those lost years.

It is a joy having her in my life, a piece of a puzzle I didn't know was missing. Now that she is in my life, I don't understand how it was possible we didn't know each other before. The connection between us was so strong right away, that when we met, I recognized her in a way that went beyond meeting someone for the first time who might or might not be related to you. Instinctively, I could feel we were for sure related. I recognized her as one of my people, same tribe, whatever you'd like to call it.

Later, when she confessed to struggling with drinking, I knew the connection was even stronger than I thought. I took her to her first meeting. It was a moment when everything made sense, having her, this familiar stranger, sitting next to me as we both listened to the message of recovery.

And now she is a year sober. And she calls me to tell me that just thinking about me stopped her from picking up a drink the other night. First birthdays of sobriety can be tricky like that. The urge to celebrate can mix with the urge to annihilate. It's lovely that my sister finds me to be such an inspiration. My discovery of her, of my roots, was just as inspiring. I don't know if it's one of the things that keeps *me* from drinking, but I think so. There would be no journey of such self-discovery, or the joy of meeting someone like her, if I were lying passed out on a couch.

I don't think about my sobriety all the time but sobriety gave me a bridge to human beings. True, I'm not praying and begging and working to stay sober any more. But once I stopped drinking, I was able to sanitize my brain so used to being obscured in booze, toxicity. Being clear-headed helped me to not obsess over all these self-conscious emotions I have. It used to be clenched fists; now it's exhaling. Before it was a total alienation; now it's talking with people like my half-sister, opening my heart. Now it's being able to inspire someone and finding inspiration in others.

And the connections get deeper. The more you open up, the more others open up to you. My getting sober got me my children back, too. I am no longer a ghost dad. Today, we communicate on levels I didn't think were possible. They know my pain and I know theirs. We've been to a war as a family and we came back, wounded but ready to mend.

Sometimes when we talk, I remember my own adoptive father—the long silences as we drove in the car and my mind spinning, trying to figure out topics to discuss and not being able to find any I would deem interesting enough. Feeling like a failure again because I wasn't able to entertain him with a conversation. Not that he had ever demanded it. He was a quiet guy by nature, but to me, his silence signaled that there was something wrong with me, that perhaps I wasn't worth talking to.

So here I am with my children, and it's exactly the opposite. I know their hopes, their dreams. I am able to be present for them. It is all so precious to me because I almost lost it.

Today, my mantra is simply: *Life is too short.* If I were to meet you and become friends with you, reader, we would talk about real stuff, life stuff. No superficiality. What makes you happy? What troubles you? What gives you joy?

I can talk this way with others now, because I know what these things are in my life.

Once you get your life back, you discover quickly that there's no time for squandering energy. My half-sister and I became a family almost instantly because I was able to be present for her. I wouldn't have been able to do that before. Even with dozens of people in my life, I couldn't really see myself reflected in them.

I can see myself in people now. And there are times, too, when I meet people and can tell that they see me— really *see* me. There's really no greater joy than to know you're being acknowledged. It's the opposite of the microscope I used to be under. It's not about being inspected, judged—it's about relating. A microscope is a tool, a machine that merely conveys the image, but being seen means that the judgment is minimal and that we understand one another on a human level. Beyond that, just delusions, dreams, lies.

Phenomenal

My life is phenomenal. When I write *"my life is phenomenal,"* this is not me bragging about material things or vacations or the beautiful house I live in. Or the lake. Sometimes it's not even about my family, my children and my wife and my close friends and all the love I now get to feel. It's not about my work. It's not about discovering my past and making true friends.

Or rather, it's about all those things, but most specifically, it's about being able to experience all those things consciously and fully. I've had most of those things in my life—vacations, houses, a loving family, friends— but I wasn't there. I was in the other world, where nothing would get through the veil of alcohol.

True, there were moments I felt euphoric, in love with life, but even then, even at the peak of that kind of happiness, there was a barrier nothing could penetrate. Who was this guy who was me? The guy at war with himself? The same conundrum, always. And then sometimes, there were thoughts of such despair, I was going mad from my dissociation. Nothing seemed real. My phenomenal life back then was not phenomenal. It was a movie of a life, something I merely watched and sometimes puzzled over. I wasn't there. I was a hologram of myself.

Today, I'm able to be conscious; it's almost as if I developed an extra sense. I don't know what that sense is. It has to do with Reality, again, with my ability to stay in the moment, whether for myself or somebody else.

Club Limbic

According to one definition, the limbic system "is a complex set of brain structures located on both sides of the thalamus, right under the cerebrum." It supports a variety of functions, including adrenaline flow, emotion, behavior, motivation, long-term memory, and olfaction. Emotional life is largely housed in the limbic system, and it has a great deal to do with the formation of memories. In other words, and most pertinent to our discussion, the limbic system is responsible for motivation, emotion, learning, and memory.

I have this fantasy. There should be something beyond existing fellowships for me and for others who have been traumatized, people who are overly affected by self-conscious emotions through abandonment, betrayal, and Shame. There should be something for people like me who have developed an appreciation for deep conversations and friendships that will feel instantly right. Some kind of utopian, ultra-safe place.

I picture a place, maybe decorated in wood with lots of space and light coming through, an opposite to the infamous church basement where so many 12-step meetings tend to occur. Tables with people gathered around them. The rules not imposed but instinctively understood. No interrupting, attentive listening, simple manners of being civilized and friendly.

My fantasy extends further. I'd like to open this club. I'd call it Club Limbic. A place where you could talk about your demons—shame, feeling abandoned, coping—but not only that. A place where you could talk about your aspirations, inspirations, where the ideas could flow freely. Alive, lively meditation. It would fulfill this void we have now in our society because of so many distractions. It would be unplugging from the world that demands for you to keep going no matter what. A haven.

I can't say if I'm joking, because the fantasy seems so desirable. How wonderful it would be to advertise that in Club Limbic we provide a warm and welcoming meeting place for men, women, and children who need a safe place to revel in their emotions, and not be afraid of showing their true selves.

I can picture it all. I can't picture God but I can picture a utopian fantasy where broken people can become whole again, together.

* * * * *

When folks seek recovery, especially those who have suffered trauma, they don't have trust in other people and many have severe abandonment and attachment issues. They're extremely vulnerable without their proven coping mechanism—in my case, alcohol. As 12-step program members, some might get further shamed by being told to shut up, to not think, to destroy their ego. We are told that we're powerless over alcohol, which is true. But we are also told that we're powerless over our thoughts (ourselves!).

This feels inauthentic, as solitude and depending on ourselves is literally what has kept us alive for so long. When we're told relying upon ourselves is what got us to 12-step meetings—selfishness, self-centeredness, ego, our will not his, and so on—we become hopeless and find that we again have nowhere to turn, thus furthering the shame spiral and attendant feelings of isolation. Not feeling included in 12-step programs then feels like insanity, which, if some program members are to be believed, can result only in institutions or death.

If we somehow manage to stick around and get to the third step—"Made a decision to turn our will and our lives over to the care of God as we understood God"—we're told we need to find a God outside of ourselves to trust and to turn our thoughts and actions over to. The only loser we can trust at that point is our damaged self. Our vulnerability is punished with shame when we're told we're doing it wrong, that we're not doing enough.

But if we ever strengthen ourselves, we can create healthy boundaries first, then finally become emotionally available to others. There remains, however, suspicion that others don't have our backs, so lots of effort needs to go into finding people we can trust.

* * * * *

I'm not naive. Whether it's in 12-step rooms or else-where, there are bad people who will ruin things for the rest of us. There are no absolute guarantees anywhere. There is no Club Limbic. And even in Club Limbic, how long would it take before a predator would qui-etly sneak into its midst? But you'll have to find your place, even if it's imperfect. Eventually, you'll have to trust someone and believe it's okay to open yourself up to another human being and to the world.

Not a TV Show

In my line of work, as an addiction professional, I get to see people at their worst and at their best. When I drank, I watched the TV show *Intervention* to feel better about myself. I judged the junkies, the thieves. I had pity but no compassion. It was just a TV show.

It is not just a TV show.

With the screen removed, the TV show becomes reality. I see sorrow and despair and the tears, right in front of my very eyes. Parents desperate to rescue their child intent on killing herself with drugs. I have children. I cannot imagine witnessing them slicing themselves open with needles or drowning themselves in alcohol. Because I know this would lead to their imminent demise, a death like my mother's if they didn't get it the way I got it.

I was just lucky. There was no godly intervention. There was a coming to and a survival instinct that kicked in so hard, I landed right on my face and then managed to get up. But who knows if my children would be lucky enough to notice they were going to perish if they were addicts and using? Not everyone gets as scared as I did.

I watch my children go through difficult times and it's hard not to try to intervene, but they're adults now and independent. The best I can do is offer some suggestions, and nine times out of ten, they'll be willing and ready to listen to them.

And I am aware of the statistics, and I share them with them. My daughter is four times more likely to become an alcoholic than an average woman, my son nine times. Their lineage is complicated; they have genes in them that can go off like time bombs.

So I understand the people who come to me.

The father whose son doesn't believe in treatment.

The mother who says her son doesn't care.

The mother who lies to herself—because of denial—about her daughter, who says she's got it under control.

The daughter who says recovery is pointless anyway, as we're all going to die.

There's nothing you can do for someone who doesn't believe in treatment. It's not going to work. It's like trying to convince a person that he's a frog. To an addict in total denial, intervention is nothing more than an interruption in a drug flow.

What can I do? What can *we* do? I don't have the answers. I have some answers. Tough love doesn't work; throwing a kid on the street might be akin to manslaughter. It's not enabling to love someone unconditionally. Addicts need safety; they need to be able to trust. A rehab boot camp is not the answer. Fear is only a motivator for so long.

Addicts don't need more torment. They spend their entire lives trying to annihilate themselves. What they need are arms that will hold them and some sense of security. Security, for an addict, is a springboard to life.

*****

There are many success stories, too. That's another phenomenal thing about my life: I get to see eyes fill with light, zombies turning into beautiful human beings. A scowling mute becoming a chatterbox full of smiles. A mother getting a visit from an estranged daughter. A hug that looks like clinging onto a raft. I get overwhelmed with joy; I am the luckiest man in the world to be able to witness these moments.

It's watching something akin to miracles on an everyday basis.

And I know that dogma has no place in recovery. Evolution does. We cannot be static and satisfied with lines memorized from the *Big Book* or the tenets of SMART Recovery (Self-Management and Recovery Training; an alternative to 12-step meetings). Everyone is different. Yes, addicts share common traits—confusion about reality being the main one—but there's more to people than just 12 steps, 12 signs of the zodiac.

Every day, my mind opens a little more and I notice that everything is a part of a whole. The unwilling addict, and the one who gets to live. The Parallel Universes. It can go either way once you take that first drink. It does nothing for you; it does everything for you. And if it does everything for you, it will kill you or you will get to be reborn.

* * * * *

I'm a member of a 12-step program, even though I no longer subscribe to some of its members' shaming techniques, but I have also come to terms with being okay with that. You know why I'm a member even though I've never found God? Because the only requirement for membership is the desire to stop drinking. That's it.

I will probably never go back to torturing myself with finding my place in mainstream recovery. I go to those meetings, but I will always be somewhat uncomfortable there, although I will be quiet about it. There's no point in trying to convince a believer into not believing, same as it was for me. Fitting round pegs into square holes is a frustrating process for both the pegs and the square holes.

For all its questionable aspects, participation has taught me something that is invaluable in my relentless pursuit of Reality and connection. It has taught me how to find people with whom I can develop common language and with whom I can be perceptive, empathetic, even. I'm not a fan of the word "gift," but it's a gift to be able to stand in the corner at a loud party, somewhere, and have a deep conversation with another human being. The Yacht Club, for example—I still go, although my involvement is nowhere close to what it used to be. But I go because that was and still is a part of my life.

Except this time, I just talk to people. I want to relate to them. I can do that without booze now.

* * * * *

Everyone is walking around with something heavy; there's often pain under fake smiles. We are complex creatures and so many of us live in Parallel Universes similar to what I've lived. Doesn't have to be addiction. Could be grief, lost love…anything really. I try to treat others gently and be there for them.

It's not an intellectual concept. Rather it's a feeling, an overwhelming sense of peace and love I feel for another human being because we are connecting. It's true that you can't do that with everyone, have this deep connection, the sort of conversations that will open minds and hearts. And so what?

You can't expect everybody to understand you. Life would be boring if all it consisted of was applause. There are people who challenge what we believe in, and that's okay, too. I think of polite Christmas dinners with my in-laws, the horror on their faces when in the past, I brought up something difficult.

With those who can open up, my desire is to give away those feelings I have about being secure in the world, about seeing the world clearly without a veil. You cannot do that when you're afraid.

And I am less and less afraid. Of living.

Freedom

Back when I first got sober, I couldn't go sailing. It was too much—too many dark memories, and physically I couldn't do it either. I was afraid of being a sailor again. I worried that the water would be treacherous, that it would pull me in, drown me. There was perhaps some deep, hidden Pavlovian reflex in me, too, a trigger that would make me taste the first cold-warm, one-two punch. It would only last a second, but it was dangerous.

So instead, I watched my family. And it was wonderful. I loved seeing them healthy and strong: my daughter's long red hair like a triumphant flag, my son with his athletic, intuitive skill—real sailors in the making. My wife, beautiful as always, tanned and bright as the sunshine in which she basked.

I didn't feel sorry for myself that I couldn't join them. I knew now was not the time. I felt happy for them being happy. That was all. Simple.

When I did get back into sailing, it was empowering. The sober time around, it was cautious, but just as thrilling as it was in the beginning. The pull of water was friendly this time. I knew I wouldn't drown, even if my boat capsized. I didn't have to wake up sick and anxious the next day. I woke up with my mind spinning, perhaps, but the thoughts made sense and I could talk myself out of negativity. I was able to ground myself.

I was able to sit with myself and do nothing about it. I wasn't being chased by fear and I didn't have to chase a delusion.

On the boat I chased nothing. I just went forward. What else is there in life but to go forward?

On the boat, I was in control of every moment. I immediately found the balance.

I could live in the world, I thought in those first moments back on the water. I was strong and healthy. I could feel my body work from the inside, the muscles interlocking like perfectly designed cogs as I sped through. It was freedom again, similar to what it was before, but at the end of it, there was no darkness, no self-imprisonment. This was no illusion of freedom as before.

It was the real thing.

It was reality. My Reality.

Acknowledgments

My heartfelt gratitude:

To Karen for giving me life, and bequeathing to me a deep sense of the things and people to always beware of.

To Adrienne, Andrew, Rosemarie, Kristi, and Chris, for granting me the ability to feel real.

To Vicki, for allowing and encouraging me to feel less afraid of myself.

To the generous and empowering souls who validated my experiences and (oftentimes complex) perceptions.

About The Author

David B. Bohl lives to empower others. And not in the way he sees fit, but in the way that allows each individual to live his or her best way. By walking a value-centered path, he leads by example. He tries to be the best husband, father, son, brother, friend, citizen, and businessperson he can be. His life goals are centered on contributing to the lives of others using powerful, positive techniques that are firmly rooted in the pragmatic and the real.

Already heavily entwined with alcohol throughout high school, he graduated college and immediately plunged into a materialistic lifestyle. After starting as a runner on the floor of the Chicago Board Options Exchange (CBOE), the work week's adrenaline rush was as pleasurable as the weekend alcohol binges. By his thirties, he had everything he wanted—except freedom. After hitting bottom, he rebuilt...first himself, and then his life.

That process of reconstruction took him down a very different road. David earned a Masters of Addiction Studies degree and received Addiction Counseling licensing in Wisconsin, Illinois, and Minnesota. He was also granted the certification of Master Addiction

Counselor (MAC) by NAADAC (National Association for Alcoholism and Drug Abuse Counselors). Today, he is an independent addiction consultant, where he engages and empowers others as they struggle with their own or a loved one's substance use disorders and mental illnesses, and the issues particular to lifelong recovery. He hopes *Parallel Universes* will open new channels for discussions about how to assist the under-served populations of those with developmental inter-ruptions—traumatized individuals, adoptees, orphans, fostered persons, relinquished individuals, alcoholics, addicts, and their families and colleagues.

Bohl is a graduate of the University of South Florida and Hazelden Betty Ford Graduate School of Ad-diction Studies. David is a member of the National Association for Alcoholism and Drug Abuse Counselors (NAADAC), American Adoption Congress (AAC), and Concerned United Birthparents (CUB).

Today, the author lives with his wife in Milwaukee, Wisconsin. He is a current or former member of a number of national and regional sailing and yachting associations. Bohl's volunteerism through the Salva-tion Army, in the recovery community, and through a variety of sailing and yachting clubs has touched individuals from many walks of life.

Please visit www.DavidBBohl.com
for more information

CPSIA information can be obtained
at www.ICGtesting.com
Printed in the USA
FFOW04n0749060318
45480057-46203FF